Conflicts of Leadership

Good for People or Good for Business?

BENGT KARLÖF

JOHN WILEY & SONS
Chichester · New York · Brisbane · Toronto · Singapore

Original Swedish version published under the title of *Ledarskapets motsatspar–dikotomier i ett svåröverskådligt universum* (Ekerlids Förlag, Stockholm 1994).

Copyright © 1996 by Bengt Karlöf
                    Enskilda Holding Ltd
                    Barclays Bank plc
                    Limassol Business Centre
                    PO Box 1791
                    Limassol
                    Cyprus

English translation © 1996 by Alan J Gilderson
English translation published 1996 by John Wiley & Sons Ltd
Baffins Lane, Chichester,
West Sussex PO19 1UD, England
National Chichester (01243) 779777
International +44 1243 779777
e-mail (for orders and customer service enquiries): cs-books@wiley.co.uk
Visit our Home Page on http://www.wiley.co.uk or http://www.wiley.com

Other Wiley Editorial Offices

John Wiley & Sons, Inc., 605 Third Avenue,
New York, NY 10158-0012, USA

Jacaranda Wiley Ltd, 33 Park Road, Milton,
Queensland 4064, Australia

John Wiley & Sons (Canada) Ltd, 22 Worcester Road,
Rexdale, Ontario M9W 1L1, Canada

John Wiley & Sons (Asia) Pte Ltd, 2 Clementi Loop #02-01,
Jin Xing Distripark, Singapore 0512

Library of Congress Cataloging-in-Publication Data

Karlöf, Bengt, 1939–
    [Ledarskapets motsatspar. English]
    Conflicts of leadership : good for people or good for business? /
  Bengt Karlöf ; English translation, Alan J. Gilderson. — 1st ed.
      p.   cm.
  Includes bibliographical references and index.
  ISBN 0-471-96641-X (cloth)
    1. Leadership.   2. Executive ability.   I. Title.
HD57.7.K37313   1996
658.4'092—dc20
                                                  96–15011
                                                      CIP

British Library Cataloguing in Publication Data

A catalogue record for this book is available from the British Library

ISBN 0-471-96641-X

Typeset in 11/13 Palatino by Dorwyn Ltd, Rowlands Castle, Hants
Printed and bound in Great Britain by Biddles Ltd, Guildford and King's Lynn
This book is printed on acid-free paper responsibly manufactured from sustainable forestation, for which at least two trees are planted for each one used for paper production.

Contents

Preface

In nearly fifteen years as a consultant I have gradually come to recognize the high degree to which success in any activity, especially business, depends on personal factors. Objective potential for development is an essentially different phenomenon from the way that potential is actually realized. The easiest way to realize one's potential is to learn from one's own mistakes and from those of others. The idea of a mirror image of a mistake, as a rule, is an idea about what one ought to do to succeed.

As the reader may ponder over the examples of misjudgements and mistakes in various situations given in this book, it is important to bear in mind the educational aspect. Just as necessity is the mother of invention, so mistakes made in leadership are a substrate in which we can seek guidance about behaviour that leads to success.

Issues concerning leadership arise in the course of lectures, especially if the subject is strategy, business development or benchmarking. It is impossible to separate the operative content of an enterprise from leadership, except on a theoretical plane.

In the field of psychological statistics a method known as *orthogonality* is used. It is a way of reducing a large number of possible options to only a few. These options represent an amorphous mass which would otherwise be impossible to grasp in all its complexity. The method makes it possible to choose between options in a situation where too many options render a meaningful choice impossible.

I have adopted a similar approach in this book. Leadership is a complex concept which cannot be described by simple models. The variables of leadership are so great and many-faceted that they defy meaningful analysis. Like orthogonality, this book aims to reduce the many-faceted reality of leadership to a manageable number of parameters that can be described, exemplified and analysed.

In writing this book I have incurred a heavy debt of gratitude, mainly to my colleagues at Karlöf & Partners, and perhaps most of all to Mats Bodin, who persuaded me to translate my idea into action. I have also received inspiration from Lage Jonason, C-G Strandberg, Sven-Erik Sjöstrand and others, and Maja Florin has been an indispensable resource for getting the manuscript into shape.

All intellectual production begins on a platform built from other people's ideas. I therefore wish to express my gratitude to all the leaders, writers and consultants who, unknowing and unnamed, have contributed to the production of this book.

Readers' comments and views on the subject would be greatly appreciated. You are welcome to contact me by telephone, fax or letter at Karlöf & Partners, Box 70462, S-107 26 Stockholm, Sweden, telephone +46-8 698 8500, fax +46-8 698 8510.

Bengt Karlöf
Stockholm, July 1996

1
Conflicts of Leadership

The concept of leadership is exceptionally ambiguous. It does not exist as an independent educational discipline. People are educated in a distinct field of knowledge, such as law, economics or engineering, which is linked to related disciplines.

Leadership, on the other hand, crosses the boundaries of the traditional fields of knowledge such as psychology, education, economics, law, engineering, mathematics and philosophy. A discussion of leadership may also touch upon such areas as religion, ethics and ethnography.

This book deals with leadership; it does not focus on the notion of chiefdom as such. *Leader* is a Germanic word which originally meant "one who can make someone walk", while *Chief*, from the Latin *caput*, means "head". This difference will become clearer throughout the book.

AN UNEXPLORED UNIVERSE

I present leadership as a universe of disparate elements comprising traits, attitudes, types of behaviour, knowledge and situations. In this universe there are myriads of galaxies, solar systems and planets, together with a vast quantity of unexplored material consisting of black holes, antimatter and other obscure phenomena.

It has thus far proved exceedingly difficult to convey structured, analytical knowledge of such an unexplored region to the public. It is for this reason that research in the field of leadership has based itself on case studies and similar methods. One observes leaders' behaviour, and then tries to draw empirical conclusions from their actions. Leading authorities in the field, such as Sune Carlsson (Uppsala University), Henry Mintzberg (McGill University), Rosabeth Moss Kanter (Harvard University), John Caller (Harvard University), Rose Marie Stewart (Oxford University) and Mats Tyrstrup (Stockholm School of Economics) have approached the subject of leadership using this approach. One of the most striking findings of their research is the stochastic (random) element in leadership behaviour, i.e. that energy and activity are guided by impulse (e.g. telephones ring, problems have to be solved, people have to be dealt with).

DEFINITION OF LEADERSHIP

To illustrate the semantic imprecision of the term leadership I cite a question that I have put to numerous audiences at lectures and seminars: Was Adolf Hitler a good leader?

The great majority of answers are affirmative, although qualified by reservations about Hitler's unacceptable ethics and repressive methods he used. There are, however, always some respondents who, after due reflection, point out that Adolf and his associates failed in the end. So why ask the question? The answer lies in the meaning of the word leadership which is usually restricted to its charismatic aspect, i.e. the ability to arouse enthusiasm and persuade people to follow. It does not, however, embrace those traits which have to do with the success of the enterprise. In actual fact, Hitler's version of a thousand-year Reich survived for only twelve violent years which were marked by enormous suffering among his own followers and humanity at large.

The example of Hitler highlights the difficulty and imprecision in an understanding of the concept of leadership. For most people the nature and success of the enterprise are left out of their definition of leadership. As a result, training in leadership has been dominated by group dynamics and individual psychology.

SUBJECT AND OBJECT IN LEADERSHIP

In this book leadership is defined in a broad context to include its operative aspects. This, however, requires that we view leadership from a new perspective. In an earlier book, *Ledarutmaningen (The Challenge of Leadership)** we grouped the qualities of leadership into five central areas. A good leader must possess the following:

1 Helicopterability – the ability to see the whole picture in both time and space.
2 Good judgement – the ability to make sound decisions based on facts, experience and intelligence.
3 Imagination – the ability to be creative and see opportunities beyond the obvious ones.
4 Analytical ability – the deductive intelligence to draw conclusions in a logical sequence from available facts.
5 Efficiency – the ability to make decisions of crucial importance to the enterprise with high productivity.

Since then we have added a further area to the qualities of leadership:

6 Ability to win trust and inspire respect.

From these six areas we may draw the conclusion that the concepts of leader and leadership contain an important subjective element, i.e. that each individual leader acts in a certain way and displays a distinct set of character traits and behaviour patterns.

In this book I prove that leadership also contains an objective element which is the organization or whatever it is that the leader leads. This includes aspects of organized activity that can be viewed from different perspectives, including productivity, quality, time frame, strategy and organization. These aspects are often diametrically opposed to each other, and therefore are called the dichotomies, or conflicts, of leadership.

---

* Bengt Karlöf and Sven Söderberg, Ledarutmaningen, Svenska Dagbladets Förlag, Stockholm 1989.

THE DILEMMA OF LEADERSHIP

In the mid-1980s Karlöf & Partners was involved in a Problem Detection Study (PDS) poll of a large number of executives. Of the many problem areas that were identified, two stood out:

1   What can be done about people whose performance is unsatisfactory, and how shall we develop our co-workers?
2   How shall we find time to devote long-term strategic thought to our business?

This illustrates the conflict between the needs of human management on the one hand and operative management on the other. (See Chapter 3 for a further discussion of this.)

If we lived in a rational world where people always behaved in the best interests of the enterprise in any given situation, then the whole complex problem of managing people in an organization would vanish. The real world, however, is not like that. Instead, a leader's day consists of constant persuasion and manipulation of his or her co-workers – a task that is often felt to be both needlessly time-consuming and an obstacle to the process of business development. This, according to many leaders of large corporations, is one of the main reasons why they cannot find time to devote to long-term business development which should be worked on to assure future success.

The conflict between the operative content of business and the people in the organization is one of the great stumbling-blocks of leadership. People are time-consuming and, thus, encroach on the leader's use of his or her time; it is not uncommon for the human element to be such a troublesome factor that it becomes one of the principal issues of management. For example, everyone may agree that the company must cut its personnel, but when it comes to doing so, more heed is paid to individual circumstances than to the efficiency of the business. When this happens, the situation is serious. The attention of management is diverted to factors other than those which are of prime importance to the company's survival, i.e. satisfied customers and high productivity.

At a seminar on workforce reduction I was once asked the following question by an executive of a national corporation in the sultanate of Oman: "How do you go about cutting staff when all the employees are related in some way to the Chief Executive?" A delicate problem, yet not as uncommon as you may think. If you look around you in your own company you will certainly discover bonds and relationships that are apt to cause problems and sensitive situations if cutbacks should become necessary. This is one of the reasons why many companies were overmanned during the recent recession, especially on the salaried side.

I am not advocating ruthless sackings, but simply an intelligent approach to dealing with overmanning. At Karlöff & Partners we have initiated and successfully implemented a number of such projects, so we know that it is possible to combine optimization of resources with improvements in efficiency.

THE COCE MODEL

The purpose of all organized activity can be expressed very simply as: "The aim of all organized activity is to create a value which is greater than the cost of producing that value." This apparent truism contains a number of aspects that are easily overlooked, especially if either the whole is not easily recognized or your job is rewarded according to a more narrow perspective. Here lies the conflict between *value* and *productivity*. A planned economy, together with other examples of large-scale organization, has shown that high productivity alone is not enough to justify the continued existence of an enterprise. Many Russian managers are still paid according to how many employees they have or how many units they produce. Conversely, you cannot concentrate on quality to the exclusion of all else and build the Rolls-Royce equivalent of your industry without heeding the productivity aspects.

While this conflict will be discussed further in this book, it is necessary to examine the four fundamental building-blocks that form the basis of a leader's success in managing an enterprise. I am not concerned with a leader's reputation in terms of what sort of person he or she is, but in terms of how well the enterprise is run with reference to:

- Customers (users)
- Owners or equivalent principals
- Costs (productivity)
- Employees, or those who depend on the enterprise for their livelihood

These are the building-blocks of the COCE model. They are given in that order simply to form a pronounceable, easy-to-remember acronym. (Any resemblance to a certain soft drink is purely coincidental.)

On the overall level, a leader has four general demands to satisfy:

1 *Customers must be satisfied and come back for more.* All organized activity begins with customers or users who are prepared to make a financial – or other – sacrifice in order to get whatever it is that the enterprise produces.
2 *Owners must feel satisfied (with the increase in value or equivalent criterion).* The owners or principals are investors in a financial or psychological sense, and expect something in return. The nature of the return on their investment varies according to the nature of the enterprise.
3 *Costs must be acceptably low, i.e. productivity must be high.* The aim of all organized activity is to create a value which is greater than the cost of producing it. Production costs must therefore be managed in such a way that they do not threaten the continued existence of the enterprise.
4 *The personnel must be contented and motivated.* Employees and others who depend on the enterprise for their livelihood are required to produce value for the customers (users) at an acceptable cost.

There are many similarities between all types of organized activity on an abstract plane, though the logic may differ radically between, say, a religious movement and a real estate management company. One of the great challenges of leadership is to be able to recognize similarities in some respects and to cope with differences in others. Any leader must be able to handle strategic and operative issues simultaneously, while at the same time he or she must be able to deal with productivity, value, the enterprise and the people in it. There are, however, important differences between varying types of enterprise, often inherent in their respective aims. A professional leader can operate in any enterprise, but true success requires a feeling for and knowledge of the enterprise's specific logic and circumstances.

Consider the following enterprises: a church, a trade union, a limited company and a co-operative.

Customers of a church are called the congregation, and those of a trade union are called the membership.

Owners or their equivalent always exist. In a trade union or co-operative, the members are the owners. The problem of representative democracy is that the people elected to represent the owners may pursue policies contrary to those of the owners. This factor explains many of the problems that voluntary organizations run into.

Costs exist in the form of financial expenditures. The equivalent in voluntary enterprises is the time that voluntary workers give. When idealism falters, people want to be paid for what they do – a common problem in traditional voluntary organizations.

Employees exist in all enterprises, though the forms of remuneration differ. The element of idealism in many types of enterprise upsets the calculations of economic analysts for it is based on the idea that people are prepared to work without pay or for a return that cannot be measured in monetary terms.

The four parameters of the COCE model need to be emphasized as factors in the success of enterprises, though the terms are not mutually exclusive. For example, owners, customers and employees are interested parties, while costs may be composed of many elements, of which wage and salary costs for employees are the most important. Just as the term customers can symbolize creation of value, so may the term costs represent the productivity axis on an Efficiency Graph (see Figures 2.1 and 8.1). The employees are the people who do the work and the owners are, so to speak, the referees who judge the success of the enterprise.

Note that this refers to the object of leadership, not to the subject (or leader). The COCE model is based not on the personality of the leader, but on objective criteria for the success of whatever it is that he or she leads. Success in the leadership of enterprises is conditional upon paying constant attention to the four parameters of the COCE model and striking a careful balance between them.

THE COCE MODEL AND THE CONFLICTS OF LEADERSHIP

Having now identified the four parameters of leadership, we can plot them against each conflict described in this book. At the risk of being regarded as a technocrat guilty of oversimplifying a complex reality, I nevertheless attempt to structure leadership in a matrix based on the COCE model (see Figure 1.1). In each chapter which follows I relate each conflict to the four parameters of the COCE model.

Conflicts of leadership	Customers	Employees	Costs/ productivity	Owners
Value v. productivity				
Operative v. strategic leadership				
Continual improvement v. breakthrough improvement				
Fact base v. judgement				
Organic v. structural growth				
Market economy v. planned economy				
Business management v. capital management				
Thought v. action				
Good times v. bad times				

Figure 1.1 *The Fundamentals of Leadership in Relation to Some Important Conflicts.*

When reading this book you will not find the key to successful leadership, but you will see its complexity and discover new dimensions. It is not hard to prove that the universe exists as a whole. What is difficult is to observe all of the pieces which make up the whole to gain a better understanding of that universe.

It is for this reason that I have written this book. I do not believe in any miracle medicine that will make you the perfect leader, nor do I believe in any model or models that can explain all the complexities of leadership. It is indeed as complicated as it seems to many involved in it. What is important, however, is to recognize the complexity, to approach the conflicts with due humility, and to possess the energy and will to constantly improve your leadership. If you cannot or will not do that, you should seek your challenges elsewhere.

2
Value v. Productivity

The conflict between value and productivity, i.e. between the need to create value for customers and the need to do so at a low enough cost to assure the future of the enterprise and show some kind of a profit, is specially important because individual human beings, almost without exception, are better equipped to cope with one or the other of these aspects. (This idea is connected to Roger Sperry's research on the left and right hemispheres of the brain, which won him the Nobel Prize for Medicine in 1981.)

In Karlöf & Partners, we use the Efficiency Matrix to illustrate the conflict between value and productivity (see Figure 2.1). We found the matrix to be a most instructive tool, though like all matrices it may appear to present a grossly simplified picture of reality.

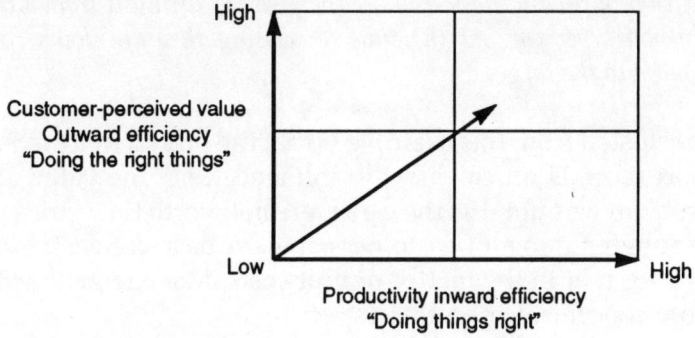

Figure 2.1   *Efficiency Matrix.*

Efficiency can be created by manipulation of either of the two axes of the matrix. Assuming a given cost structure, we can improve customer-perceived value to generate demand both quantitatively and qualitatively, i.e. to obtain a high enough price. We can also improve efficiency by reducing labour, over-head or capital costs. In reality it is very seldom a matter of either–or, but of working at influencing our position on both axes of the matrix. The order in which we tackle them – value or productivity first – may, however, be of crucial importance to the result.

One reason for the central importance of the Efficiency Matrix and the value v. productivity conflict is that *the aim of all organized activity is to create a value which is greater than the cost of producing it.*

Sequence and time allocation are key words in resolving the value v. productivity conflict. The following examples highlight this statement:

There are two kinds of inefficiency: high value with low productivity, and low value with high productivity. Cars like the Saab 9000 and Mercedes 190, both in the mid-upmarket class, are examples of the first kind.

The problem was that the cost of manufacturing, marketing and distributing those cars exceeded the price that customers were willing to pay.

In both cases the problem was diagnosed as primarily one of productivity. Saab Automobile, for example, took assembly time as an approximation of productivity and set the goal of cutting it from 110 to 40 man-hours per car. At the time of writing they are down to 45 hours, close to the target.

The conclusion from this example is that the productivity axis, in the short term, is much easier to influence than the value axis. The problem was not that the cars were not worth their price to a large enough number of customers; it was due to carelessness or lack of foresight in the matter of unit costs. Management action therefore concentrated on that aspect.

We can similarly exemplify the opposite situation, where productivity is relatively high but the value of the product is insufficient or, at worst, totally ignored. This situation is more serious, and regrettably quite common.

It is most strongly exemplified in the public sector which in many European countries operates at a loss, i.e. a national budget deficit. If we examine these budgets and start looking at what is actually produced in individual cases, the results are often astonishing. In times of acute shortage of resources the public sector continues to produce numerous peripheral services such as Fence Commissions, consumer counselling and inspection of almond paste in pastries.

It is easy for politicians to fish for votes by initiating all kinds of public service projects. Shrinking or terminating such projects is much harder, as it calls for a different type of initiative. In political decision-making, responsibility for what happens afterwards is relinquished once the decision is made. This encourages collective irresponsibility. The following is an example from my own country, Sweden:

The city of Göteborg (Gothenburg) has operated at a huge deficit for years. Like all other Swedish municipalities, it is required by law to do certain things. There are, however, other activities which it is allowed but not compelled to do – in the areas of culture, sport and recreation, for example.

Despite a large budget deficit, the city continues to do many things that it does not have to. These are subsidized by amounts equal to several times the budget deficit. Productivity in some of these activities is high, but there is no easy way to take customer-perceived value into account because no market-type relationship exists between producer and consumer. As a result, even the most competent leaders operate on only one axis of the Efficiency Matrix and thus escape the conflict.

Swedish local government offers many more "picturesque" examples of activities that are of no value to its citizens: one town in central Sweden runs chartered coach tours to Paris, and a Stockholm suburb in acute financial trouble provides a massage service for pensioners. A company studying the marine environment off Valparaiso is jointly owned by a number of Swedish municipalities, while another town owns both an electrical and household supplies shop and a sheet metal works.

PRODUCTIVITY WITHOUT UTILITY

Producing services of low value is a sin that is not confined to the public sector. We have had dealings with many companies, for example, that have incurred excessive overheads through the proliferation of central staffs. These staffs tend to justify their existence on the grounds of high productivity, i.e. a voluminous output of studies, reports, memoranda, etc.

What is interesting is that the recipients of their output often put a value on it which is lower than the actual cost of producing it. The trouble is that the value of in-house production is seldom analysed. The fact is that most transactions inside a company are of the planned-economy type, in which the supply of goods and services is to someone who is not free to choose alternative suppliers. How many production units can buy personnel administration services on a free market (from outside the company)? Have you ever heard of a personnel department that went bankrupt for lack of customers?

Ambitious, performance-oriented, entrepreneurial managers should not be put in charge of staffs. I have often encountered situations where such managers had enlarged their remit far beyond what was optimum for the business as a whole. That type of person should have line management responsibility where he or she can direct his or her energies outward, not inward. When raising this point at seminars, I have heard a murmur of realization from the audience. The double waste of putting energetic people in staff positions had not occurred to them. In this situation:

1   The energetic person is not given the opportunity to do what he or she does best.
2   The appointment actually damages the company, because the appointee indulges in empire-building.

Issues of productivity, generally speaking, are easier to handle than those of value. One reason is that engineers and accountants are usually trained in quantitative and numerical analysis, which can be readily applied to productivity.

Costs of various kinds are relatively easy to quantify, whereas customer-perceived value is not. Let us therefore briefly

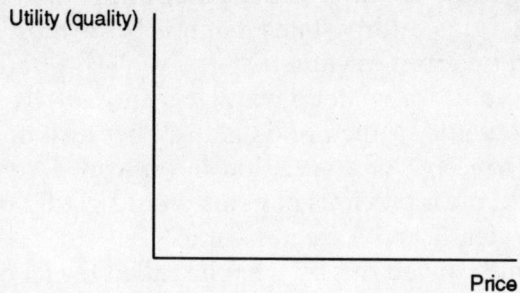

Figure 2.2 *Value Graph.*

consider the value axis of the Efficiency Matrix. Figure 2.2 illustrates the components of this axis: utility or quality in relation to price.

It is important to note that productivity, expressed as the cost of producing a service, is equal to the price paid by the receiving unit when the service is delivered within an organization. Thus in a planned economy, productivity is equal to price. This is not the case in a market economy, where, on the one hand, the price may be much higher than productivity requires and may thus yield a handsome surplus. On the other hand, the price that the customer is willing to pay may be lower; this leads to a loss, and hopefully to corrective action.

VALUE THEORY

The subject of value theory has a long history. Aristotle raised a question with ethical overtones that economists have pondered for some time: "Why is it that the most useful things in existence have the lowest value on the market, while some of the least useful command the highest prices?"

Many economists puzzled over the difference between use value and exchange value well into the nineteenth century. Whereas bread and potable water are useful and relatively cheap, silk and diamonds are not particularly useful, yet very expensive.

Adam Smith thought on the same question. The riddle of use value and exchange value was not to be solved for another century when the concept of marginal utility was created. The theory of marginal utility states that it is is the most *desirable* use or need that determines value.

The use value of water is low because of its abundance, whereas the value of diamonds is high because of their rarity. One could conceive of a situation in an arid desert where the brightest and most precious of gems would gladly be traded for a glass of water. Scarcity creates value.

Adam Smith solved this by what he called the labour theory of value. This means simply that the value of an asset is measured by the amount of labour for which that asset can be exchanged.

The theory of marginal utility, like many conceptual break-throughs, arose at roughly the same time in a number of places. The economist to whom the development of the theory is attributed was Herman Heinrich Gossen (1810–58). Gossen expounded his theory in a book which, unfortunately, did not sell very well. He collected the remaindered copies, made a bonfire of them and died a disappointed and embittered man, totally unaware of his posthumous fame.

The essence of marginal utility theory can be expressed thus: "The marginal utility of an article is the increment to total utility or satisfaction generated by the most recently purchased unit of the article in question."*

There are two important corollaries to the theory which are relevant to the law of supply and demand:

1   The law of diminishing marginal utility states that marginal utility to the consumer diminishes with increasing consumption of a given product.
2   The consumer tends to maximize the total utility of his or her consumption by distributing purchases of goods in such a way that the marginal utility of buying one type of goods is equal to the marginal utility of buying any other type of goods.

Customer-perceived value, as we have noted, is much harder to analyse than productivity. Many traditional market surveys

* Richard T. Gill, *Modern Economics*.

analyse only attitudes which do not match the actual behaviour of consumers when the time comes to make a buying decision. In recent years, however, a number of new analytical techniques have been developed which predict actual behaviour much more accurately.

THE CONCEPT OF QUALITY IN RELATION TO CUSTOMER-PERCEIVED VALUE

The current topicality of quality issues in industry and commerce is a sign that managements are taking a greater interest in value which is used here in the sense of a function of utility and price. The term quality, however, is confusing as it has two different meanings: on the one hand, quality is associated with the zero-defect philosophy and quality costs, matters which in the first instance affect productivity. On the other hand, quality is related to customer perceptions which in one way or another affect the value that a company creates and thus influence the revenue side. Figure 2.3 illustrates this interrelationship.

Norm-related quality, i.e. conformity with production specifications, affects both quality costs and value. Quality costs, in turn, influence productivity which shows up on the cost side of the profit-and-loss account. Customer-perceived quality enhances value which can be translated into either a larger volume of sales or a higher price per unit sold. In the first instance there are Experience Curve effects, i.e. unit cost falls with cumulative volume. This is represented by the broken line pointing right in Figure 2.3. Customer-perceived quality mainly affects the income side of the profit-and-loss account.

These two aspects of quality are often left unexplained, with the result that they are often confused. At Karlöf & Partners we consistently use the term "value-related quality" which means that a given quality factor is set in relation to the customer's willingness to pay. The same concept can also be called value analysis which has its origins in the mechanical engineering industry. Conceptually, however, value analysis can be applied equally well to production of services. If we dismantle a given configuration of products and/or services into its component

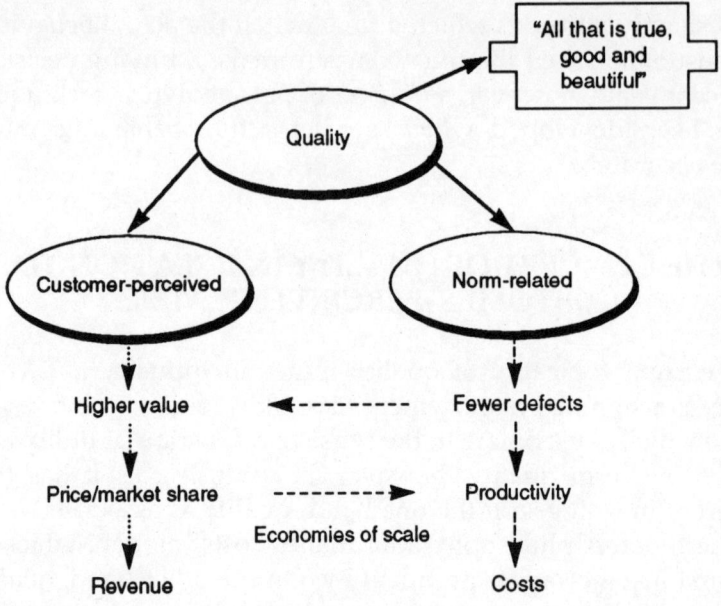

Figure 2.3   *The Two Dimensions of Quality.*

parts and try to find out what value customers put on each of the parts, we can acquire a good picture of their willingness to pay for the various parts and for the whole. By extension, this naturally means that the configuration can be altered to maximize customer satisfaction.

Failure to relate quality to willingness to pay can lead you into fundamental error: you set out to build a "Rolls-Royce" that nobody, or at any rate too few, is willing to pay for, and you lose money on it. Let us take an example:

During the 1980s Scandinavian Airlines System (SAS) decided to broaden its offering. The management expressed the idea in terms of value for customers, but did not poll customers' preferences in advance. They assumed that the regular clientele – people travelling on business – would like the chance to purchase a whole chain of services, from luggage check-in at the hotel, ground transportation, air travel with catering and ground transportation to a SAS hotel at the other end.

The concept was launched and operated for about a year, but with little success. Only then did SAS's management decide to find out how

customers valued the concept. It turned out that providing ground trans-
portation was a failure, as was ownership of hotels, since passengers chose
their hotels according to their final destinations. They did, however, appre-
ciate being able to check in their flight luggage at the hotel.

As in so many other cases, the product was offered on a basis of
intuition and vision without any analysis of customer-perceived
value until afterwards. Such ventures are frequently prompted
by the expansive ambitions of managements and staffs, who
often neglect to use available analytical instruments to study
and analyse the value aspect.

THE ESSENCE OF BUSINESSMANSHIP

The value v. productivity conflict constitutes the very essence of
what we call "businessmanship". In the present context we can
interpret the term businessmanship in its broadest sense and
apply it to all forms of organized activity. The same fundamental parameters are valid in every type of organization; thus, the
same skills are – or ought to be – in demand everywhere.

Creation of value for customers usually conflicts with productivity. The reason, of course, is that it usually costs money to
create value. The following example illustrates this conflict and
is, moreover, a true story:

In the latter half of the 1980s General Motors (GM) was deluged with
lawsuits from private persons who had bought one of the five brands of
car then in their range – Chevrolet, Pontiac, Oldsmobile, Cadillac and
Buick. This was before the launch of the new Saturn model.

The background to the lawsuits was that GM had decided to concen-
trate engine manufacturing to a single factory, which happened to be
part of the Chevrolet Division. When customers who had bought a
Buick raised the hood and found "Chevrolet" stamped on the engine,
they were furious. The oft-repeated argument in these writs was, "I
paid a lot of money for the car of my dreams, a Buick, and now I find
they've put a cheap Chevrolet engine in it."

An inquiry into the situation revealed that GM's production engin-
eers had been able to make substantial cost savings by using the same

engine in the basic versions of all five models. A saving of 5.50 dollars per engine, multiplied by the number of basic models manufactured, worked out at an astronomical total saving. The management was faced with the need to strike a balance between customer-perceived value and an opportunity to rationalize. In this case, their decision turned out to be a bad one. It would have been so easy to change the die in the engine block castings.

Volkswagen (VW) in Europe offers an example of the opposite approach. They use joint production of parts for all their marques, so under the hood of a SEAT built in Spain you will find an engine stamped Audi, VW and SEAT. This enhances the value of the downmarket car, but what do Audi owners think?

For many people, the choice of a car is a way of expressing their identity. In that kind of situation, corporate managements must weigh subtle value-for-customer aspects such as individuality, prestige, personality and lifestyle against savings on engine production in dollars and cents. The balance that is struck symbolizes the hard decisions of businessmanship between the value and productivity axes of the Efficiency Matrix.

It is easy to find more illustrative examples of the conflict between value and productivity. An airline's ambition to optimize productivity may cause it to buy a large aircraft such as Boeing 747 jumbo jets which operate at a low cost per passenger-mile. This, however, means reducing the frequency of departures, which is one of the most decisive factors in travellers' choice of airline.

Neglecting value for customers in favour of productivity is one of the major pitfalls of leadership. One of my motives for writing this book has been to encourage leaders in business, public administration and other organizations to weigh the interests of value against those of productivity with greater care.

VALUE V. PRODUCTIVITY IN RELATION TO THE COCE MODEL

The link between value and *customers* is easy to understand. Value is harder to analyse than productivity, but methods are available to do so and the effort ought to be made. High productivity benefits the customer because it improves your chances of keeping prices down, thereby enlarging the numerator in the value fraction.

Profit for *owners* is generated by the company's ability to maintain a high level of value in relation to costs. By achieving high productivity one can keep costs low in relation to the value created for customers, thereby generating a surplus. In addition, owners naturally feel successful if the company they own manufactures attractive products and can sell them at a good profit.

Costs of various kinds are the major factor that affects productivity. One of the difficulties lies in distinguishing between "good" and "bad" costs. Good costs are those which contribute to enhanced customer-perceived value or higher productivity, while bad ones are those incurred by corporate deadwood and bureaucracy.

Employees are always happier working in companies that give their customers good value and manage to combine this with high productivity – i.e., companies which are profitable. Success in achieving this combination provides room for manoeuvre, giving scope for creativity and personal initiative.

Try this exercise:

Make a list of three indicators of the productivity of your operation. Then make another list of three indicators of customer-perceived value.

Review your ten most recent decisions, major or minor, in detail and try to relate those decisions to the six indicators you have listed. Did the decisions mainly have to do with productivity or with value for customers?
How do the two axes influence each other in your operation?
Do you regularly work on both axes of the Efficiency Matrix or do you concentrate on one of them?

3
Operative Leadership v. Strategic Leadership

Let us consider two extremes: the first is the individual who seems to suffer from short-term performance anxiety and must do things now, without delay and often without stopping to think. The second is the individual who gets bogged down in hazy visions and is incapable of taking immediate action. This chapter is about the conflict between operative leadership, as suggested in the first instance, and strategic leadership, as in the second.

The confusion in this area leads me to define these terms: by operative leadership I mean action taken at the present time or in the immediate future with a view to improving this year's bottom line or its equivalent. Strategic leadership is a matter of present action taken to assure future success, however that success may be measured.

Figure 3.1 represents a rough sketch of the issues normally dealt with under the headings of strategic and operative efficiency respectively. Quality falls under both the operative and strategic headings, depending on whether the term is used to refer to zero-defect production or customers' perceptions of value, i.e. price-related quality.

A NEW VIKING AGE

In the 1980s action and initiative were prized at the expense of thoughtful reflection. Tom Peters coined phrases like "Try it, fix

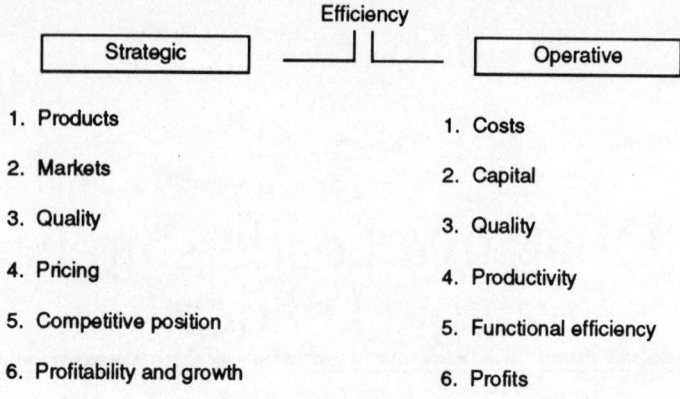

Figure 3.1 *Issues of Strategic and Operative Efficiency.*

it, do it", which major corporations adopted as their slogans. Decisiveness and swift action appealed to the macho mind, making the more reflective, laid-back and maybe hesitant types look like inferior leaders. In Scandinavia numerous and often foolhardy Viking expeditions were launched to all corners of the world, encouraged by undervalued and deregulated currencies.

The cult of operative action expressed itself not only in productivity and customer-perceived value but also in both organic and structural growth. Companies bought up other companies and set up foreign subsidiaries: frenzied, chaotic diversification was rife.

STRATEGIC SKILLS

Let us first take a more detailed look at the question of strategy. The essence of our definition of strategic issues is that they are long-term in nature, but call for action in the short term. Strategy requires:

1 An appreciation of global trends.
2 The ability to discern the need for changes to follow the trends.
3 Possession of the necessary tools for change management.
4 A combination of fact base and judgement.
5 Leadership and communication.

It follows from this that strategic issues are closely linked with investment, which is defined as *a present financial sacrifice made for the sake of future gain.*

If we want to improve this year's bottom line we can easily axe all activities aiming at future success, thereby making the enterprise look more profitable or successful. However, the eternal balancing act performed by corporate chief executives, as well as other leaders, involves holding out enough energy and resources for future needs. With the short career cycles – 3–7 years – we see in contemporary business life, leaders are constantly beset by the temptation to neglect investment in strategic development in favour of optimizing success during their own terms of office.

A further complication arises in that investments in strategic development show up most prominently on the cost side of the profit-and-loss account. Economists traditionally treat investment as a depreciable asset on the balance sheet, but in this age of knowledge-based companies and information technology, investments are more often of a kind that cannot be capitalized in a balance sheet.

Strategic management generally involves a heavy element of the latter type of investment. A company needs to budget costs for salaries, consultants, studies and analyses to acquire input for long-term development decisions. In other cases there may be a need to negotiate, exploit, search for suitable candidates for acquisition, study synergies, etc.

Long-term ambitions are frequently inspired by motives other than the greater good of the enterprise. Here we must distinguish between true and stated motives, which may in fact differ considerably. The Swedish automotive company Volvo is a case in point:

From the beginning of his appointment as Volvo's CEO in 1972, Pehr G. Gyllenhammar gave the company's executives and staff the impression that cars no longer enjoyed top priority. His pronouncements that Volvo must free itself from its heavy dependence on passenger cars was interpreted as a deprecation of that business unit, though such was not his intention.

In his actions as CEO, Mr Gyllenhammar repeatedly demonstrated his relative lack of interest in cars, for example, by using them as a transactional currency in planned deals with the governments of Norway (oil) and France (the Renault Group).

For twenty years, Volvo's strategic energies were mainly devoted to "balancing risks in the portfolio", according to official statements. This meant that the attention of top management was distracted and no longer focused upon passenger cars. Like other big automotive groups, Volvo diversified into other technologies – for example, aero engines – but also into such areas as pharmaceuticals, foods and leisure goods. It was also indicative that top executives in the organization were rewarded according to the year's profits, not according to long-term product development.

A lot of people today, both inside and outside Volvo, are wondering how its passenger car business would have developed if it had remained at the focus of strategic planning. Ten years ago, for example, Volvo built substantially more cars than BMW. One is tempted to speculate what Volvo's volume of sales would have been today if vehicle development, especially of the 400 and 800 series had been accelerated and if Volvo had gone in for vans, 4-wheel drive, etc.

It is true that Volvo has made a lot of money, but there are many who feel that it has been made at the expense of the organic development of the company's core business, specifically passenger cars. At the time of writing, this view dominates Volvo's strategic focus under its new management and new Board.

ASPECTS OF SYNERGIES

The field of strategy was long dominated by concepts like synergy, resource allocation and risk-spreading. Synergy is a term that is often used to justify expansion based on entirely different motives. The most common types of synergy are:

1   Economies of scale from shared resources in the form of joint functions such as purchasing, production, sales force or research and development (R & D).
2   Transfer of knowledge between functions, e.g. marketing, R & D.
3   Lines of business in which similarities in trade logic enable culture and leadership to be transferred from one business unit to another.

4 Shared image that enables individual business units to acquire added status in the eyes of customers by being identified with other, well-reputed business units.
5 Vertical integration, which can add value in some cases: it
   can mean better contact with end users, stability in business
   relations or more dependable access to products, technologies and services.
6 Greater attractiveness to customers where the combined offerings of two or more business units represent more value
   to customers than each of their offerings separately.

All strategic thinking naturally proceeds from a need for efficiency and assurance of survival. The origin of business
strategy is generally dated to the 1920s when the commanding
officer of the Wright Patterson United States Air Force (USAF)
base near Dayton, Ohio demonstrated the correlation between
long production runs and high productivity.

This officer proved that the unit cost of any given component fell
by roughly 25% every time the accumulated volume of production
doubled. The correlation was dubbed the Experience Curve, and it
assumed fundamental importance in thinking on the subject of
strategy. The Experience Curve is composed of a number of effects
arising out of large-scale production. For most people, it is mainly
associated with learning effects of the following kinds:

1 *Productivity of labour.* When workers repeat a given task, it is
   gradually performed with ever-greater efficiency.
2 *Work organization.* The organizational set-up is adjusted in
   the direction of greater specialization, or alternatively
   restructured.
3 *Manufacturing process.* New inventions and improvements in
   the process.
4 *Altered labour-capital balance.* As an operation expands, it may
   grow more capital-intensive and less labour-intensive.
5 *Product standardization.* The benefits of the Experience Curve
   cannot be realized to the full without product standardization.
6 *Technical specialization.* As the production process develops,
   specialized equipment is procured.

7   *Redesign.* As experience accumulates, the product can be re-
designed to economize on materials, energy and labour.
8   *Economies of scale.* In analytical terms, economies of scale are
actually a distinct phenomenon and can be obtained independently of the Experience Curve. Economy of scale simply
means that a fixed cost is distributed among a larger number
of units.

The first half of the twentieth century was an age of mass production and mass consumption which heavily influenced the
breakthrough of the Experience Curve concept. The logic of the
concept was as follows:

1   Large volumes are naturally desirable because unit costs
diminish with increasing volume.
2   The route to larger volume lies in increasing one's market
share at the expense of one's competitors.
3   One thus achieves a cost advantage that can be utilized in
one of two ways:
    (a) to earn a lot of money and thereby feel successful and
    financially strong;
    (b) to cut prices, sell larger volumes and thus earn more
    money or take a bigger market share.

These ideas have long dominated strategic thinking and are
often, though not always, relevant. The growing proportion of
services relative to goods in commerce, together with the inertia
inherent in mass production, has tended to reduce the importance of the Experience Curve. A further factor is the increasing
importance of customer-perceived value in an age of affluence.

There was not much need for businessmanship in a world of
short supply and excess demand. What was necessary to be
successful was mathematical logic. The requirement was for efficiency in production, administration and distribution. The
needs of mass production, however, conflict with those of cus-
tomization; this is one of the crucial issues of businessmanship.

Another motive for striving for growth and high market
shares is based on the human urge to expand, without which the
world today would have looked very different. Among the chief

explanatory factors in the tremendous advance of Western Europe since the Mercantile Age were the decay of feudal obedience-conditioning and the worship of God through work according to the teachings of Martin Luther. These factors allowed for, and unleashed, human initiative.

STRATEGY AND VISION

Assurance of future success for the enterprise is the objective of business strategy, whose principal component elements are the following:

- Products
- Markets
- Competitive advantages

The most important competitive advantages can almost always be related to high productivity or high customer-perceived value. Under those headings one can then list factors such as capital commitment, product development, and so on.

The term vision has come to be widely used in recent years in the context of business strategy. Its true definition is something seen in a dream or, as the Swedish neurophysiologist David Ingvar has called it, a memory of the future. Vision and strategy overlap in that they both describe a desirable future state of affairs, though a vision can be said to view the future of an enterprise in a wider perspective than strategy. Whereas strategy is largely a matter of plans for the future and their expected results, a vision is less specific on the surface level while giving more information about the shape and feel of things to come and about why the future it depicts comprises elements that are important to the organization and the people working in it.

Most business strategies are based on objective analyses of external conditions and facts in relation to internal strengths and weaknesses. Visions take account of all this, but are based on less predetermined and tangible premisses. Instead, visions usually embrace motivating factors such as the needs and aspirations of people in the organization and the place of the enterprise in a wider social context.

Leaders of organizations should concern themselves with both strategies and visions. Strategies should not be a surrogate for visions. The technocrat's urge to tag everything with letters and numbers must not be allowed to overshadow each individual's desire to dream of the future.

OPERATIVE SKILLS

Visions, strategies, far-sightedness and business development have at times overshadowed the apparently trivial hands-on operative skills that every enterprise needs. It is a tragedy of European development that the politicians and officials responsible for public business have largely failed to acquire operative skills and to have learned how to make painful decisions in times when resources are no longer expanding. Many of the phenomena associated with times of prosperity breed a cultural pattern and a style of leadership that are inefficient in times of adversity. At such times, operative skills are a commodity in short supply.

Chief executives appointed in hard times are often skilled operators and somewhat technocratic; they are at a loss when an upturn comes, giving scope for action of a more visionary and strategic kind.

Conversely, leaders appointed in good times are frequently visionaries who lack the ability to wield the operative axe when the going gets rough. This paradoxical situation is shown in Figure 3.2.

	Visionary	Technocrat/operator
Boom	Ill-equipped to cope with coming downturn	Not very good at business development, but will be an asset when the downturn comes
Recession	Short on operative skills, but will be an asset when the upturn comes	Copes well in tough times, but not good at exploiting opportunities for expansion

Figure 3.2   *Executive Types in Boom Times and Recessions.*

The same situation applies to politicians who have been, and to some extent still are, responsible for the national economy. Most of them grew up in the expansive society of the post-war reconstruction period. They have grown accustomed to being seen as the givers of all good gifts, and thus feel acutely uncomfortable in a situation that makes diametrically opposed demands.

There is nothing wrong with generalizations as such. It is perfectly permissible to state that Italians are more likely than Swedes to have dark hair. The mistake that many people make is to attribute the general to the individual: "You are Italian, so your hair must be dark." We may thus allow ourselves to generalize, but we must beware of overdoing it.

In the previous chapter we dealt with the conflict between customer-perceived value and productivity. A monopoly such as a national postal service in Europe can disregard customer-perceived value and concentrate on optimizing its productivity. Taken to extremes, this would mean that it concentrated all operations to a single General Post Office in the capital city where everybody would have to go to collect their mail. Not at all customer-friendly, but definitely the most productive arrangement.

Another aspect is that operative skills are exercised within a time frame which may vary. One could in fact claim that a high level of operative skill compared to competitors constitutes a strategic competitive advantage. Let us consider the example of Toyota:

Toyota has adopted an intelligent analytical approach: combining customer-perceived value where appropriate with high productivity where that is the prime consideration. Using modern value analysis, lean production and continual improvement, Toyota has succeeded in optimizing its position on both axes of the Efficiency Matrix. Custom variation is offered wherever possible without unduly hampering productivity. High productivity takes over where it is needed to offer customers a low enough price. For the past twenty years, Toyota has succeeded in optimizing quality parameters and productivity factors in a way that has astonished the world.

LONG TERM, SHORT TERM

As in so many other respects, individual human beings differ in their ability to cope with operative and strategic problems. Though this may seem too obvious to mention, awareness of one's own limitations can be a strength in itself. Strategic and operative abilities are respectively linked with long and short time frames.

However, as we have seen, strategic issues have an important short-term dimension, while operative skills have a long-term one. Figure 3.3 illustrates the four possible situations.

The short-term dimension of strategic issues is that action must be taken and financial sacrifices made at the present time to assure success in the future. Thinking about and planning strategy are activities that consume management time, which is naturally a resource. Strategic issues thus have an important short-term aspect which often involves current-account investment.

The long-term aspects are inherent in the very nature of strategy. Products and markets are chosen and developed to create competitive advantages. The action is taken now, but brings results in the future.

The short-term dimension of operative issues is equally obvious. By definition, they refer to factors which will influence the bottom line this year or in the next few years.

The long-term dimension of operative issues can be exemplified by companies like Toyota in the automotive industry, American Airlines and British Airways in civil aviation, or

	Strategic	Technocrat/operator
Short term	Current-account investment	Greater efficiency
Long term	Choice of products and markets	Competitive advantage through high productivity

Figure 3.3 *The Long and Short Term in Strategic and Operative Issues.*

Swedish Telia and Dutch PTT in telecommunications. All of them are skilled at meeting customers' wishes at all times within the framework of their respective corporate missions. By acquiring an operative competence that is better than their competitors' they have, in my opinion, gained a competitive lead that will be hard to overcome.

The telecom companies, for example, have focused their research and development on the role of the operator, systematically identifying all the advantages of digitalization and thereby achieving operative superiority. Like leaders in many other industries, they use benchmarking, business process reengineering (BPR) and other analytical techniques to map out potential areas of improvement.

The competitive advantages may seem modest, but according to all experience they lead to cost advantages that are crucially important in competition. This will be discussed further in Chapter 4.

OPERATIVE SKILLS AND STRATEGIC SKILLS IN RELATION TO THE COCE MODEL

One of the challenges of business lies in understanding *customers'* needs better than they do themselves. Customers can never express needs that they are unaware of. Their attention must be drawn to new techniques which make it possible to satisfy their needs. One of the strategic challenges of business is being able not only to satisfy known present needs, but also to understand needs and thus to discover better ways of satisfying them.

Owners who vote with their feet put more value on operative than on strategic skills. Such owners are apt to sell their shares as soon as the level of profits starts to dip. It is thus a delicate task to persuade owners to endorse strategic measures that cost money right now but are expected to yield a profit in the future.

Today's *costs* can be tomorrow's revenues if they are well managed. Action that has a negative effect on short-term profitability can pay long-term dividends which are well worth the sacrifice. In cases where present expenditure cannot be capitalized on the balance sheet but must be booked as a cost, it is up to the leader to explain the incurred costs to owners and employees in such a way that they accept the wisdom of the expenditure.

Great care must be taken to explain the nature of this conflict – which is not at all easy to appreciate – to *employees*. You should preferably be able to assess people's ability not only to achieve immediate operative efficiency, but also to take appropriate action today for the sake of future success. This calls for judgements which by their very nature are hard to quantify and measure. A crucial problem is that of devising ways to reward forward-looking strategic work as well as day-to-day operative skills.

Try this exercise:

Make a list of the three operative and three strategic problems which you consider most crucial to your enterprise today.

One way to solve operative problems is to follow good examples. Whose examples would you like to follow in each of the three operative cases?

Strategic issues have to do with investment. How do you estimate the effects of investments related to your three strategic problems on your bottom line this year and next year?

4
Continual Improvement v. Breakthrough Improvement

One might say that the American tradition of leadership is characterized by a more radical view of change management than, say, the Japanese view. In the United States they tend to talk of world class, quantum leaps or breakthroughs, whereas the Japanese emphasize change in small steps through approaches like *kaizen*, which can be freely translated as continual improvement.

A one-track search for breakthroughs can easily lead to the process of continual improvement being deprecated and neglected. Conversely, too narrow a focus on the latter can shorten one's view of the future so that pioneering advances remain undiscovered.

As in many other cases, it is not a question of either–or but of both. This makes the problem hard to deal with as the best solution in each individual case is a matter of judgement. In principle there are three steps if you want to gain a lead over your competitors and not just keep up with them:

1 Use your own inventiveness, creativity and judgement.
2 Calibrate yourself against competitors and good examples, wherever the latter may be found.
3 Reconstruct the enterprise from scratch.

Management of an enterprise tends to fall into a rut which leads to sins of omission, i.e. failure to take action that is known to be needed. One of the fundamental skills of leadership, therefore, is the ability to combine the administration of ongoing operations with a constant search for opportunities for improvement. This involves different types of process calling for different talents which are not always found in a single person. The most important talents are deduction (analysis), induction and creativity. They are defined as follows:

1   Analytical ability is based on deductive intelligence, which means a talent for dissecting a whole into its component parts and drawing a logical sequence of conclusions about the whole through examination of the parts.
2   Induction means drawing conclusions about the functions and interactions of the parts from a knowledge of the whole – understanding the value to customers of a business process, for example, and working out how each element in the process contributes to it.
3   Creativity is the ability to arrange pieces of prior knowledge in innovative ways to create successful new combinations. Creativity is an underrated intellectual process, in leadership in general and business management in particular. One reason why it is underrated is that creativity is almost invariably accompanied by a number of other traits which are frowned upon in environments where things are done by the book and intellectual self-discipline is prized.

The processes of continual improvement and systematic search for breakthrough possibilities involve intellectual exercises of all types: analysis by deduction, a holistic view with induction, and creativity.

The search for areas of continual, gradual improvement should be a permanently ongoing process in all parts of the organization. All of us, however, are creatures of habit which makes us blind to new opportunities. It is for this reason why people should change jobs from time to time, inside or outside the organization they work for, and why we have consultants. They may see things from a different perspective and can suggest new approaches, and they often – though not always – have previous experience of similar situations that can be applied to the present one.

Continual improvement means a constant search for ways to be more efficient, i.e. to enhance either customer-perceived value or productivity. The world-wide search for ways to achieve efficiency in planned-economy systems has led to a number of approaches such as total quality management (TQM), lean production, benchmarking and business process re-engineering (BPR). All of them involve two principal lines of attack: searching for gradual improvements and finding radically different ways to do things.

PROGRESS BY EXAMPLE

Benchmarking is the most effective method of achieving both continual improvement and breakthrough changes. The term is borrowed from surveying, where a benchmark is a fixed point of known location. The origins of the term derive from either the British weaving industry or the American automotive industry. In management, benchmarking means a systematic search for good examples, wherever in the world they may be found, with a view to learning from them.

At Karlöf & Partners we have used benchmarking for a number of years, both as a diagnostic instrument to identify areas for potential improvement and as a supplement to methods like TQM and BPR. People identify easily with benchmarking because it is natural to observe good examples and learn from them. The following are the advantages of benchmarking:

1 It supplies a good motive to proceed from study to action.
2 It encourages learning in decentralized systems.
3 It makes parts of the enterprise more efficient.
4 It benefits both individuals and the enterprise as a whole.
5 It is particularly suitable for organizations with a structure of local branches that all do the same kind of work.
6 It proves that improvement is possible.
7 It encourages both continual improvement and break-throughs.
8 It creates competitive advantage through competitive parity.

There are numerous examples about benchmarking that illustrate how the method has been used to accomplish radical changes. One example is as follows:

South West Airlines wanted to study turnaround times of aircraft at stations. At that time the company was just about to buy another aircraft, and had a turnaround time of 38 minutes.

South West Airlines chose as their benchmark the routines practised during pit stops in Formula 1 Grand Prix races. They drew conclusions accordingly, and by adopting a work-flow pattern with concurrent operations succeeded in shortening turnaround time from 38 to 14 minutes. The result was a radical increase in the effective capacity of their fleet which enabled them to abandon their plans to invest in another aircraft.

Light maintenance of aircraft consists of a series of operations carried out at an airport. By exactly defining the operative content of each of them, one can achieve exceptionally good comparability. Figure 4.1 shows which operations were included and which were not in the present case.

Included	Not included
• Startup procedure • Departure check • PFC • Maintenance check • X-check • Y-check • Z-check • De-icing • Ice-check • Snag item • Registration of snag item • Trouble-shooting, 24 hours • Maintenance check P • Revisions • Sick transport • Hangar towing • Towing assistance • Check planning	• Cleaning • Washing (outside) • Fuelling • Refuelling procedure • Heating/climate • Water/sanitation • Loading/deloading • Push-back • W-check • Other letter checks

Figure 4.1 *Operations in Light Maintenance of Aircraft.*

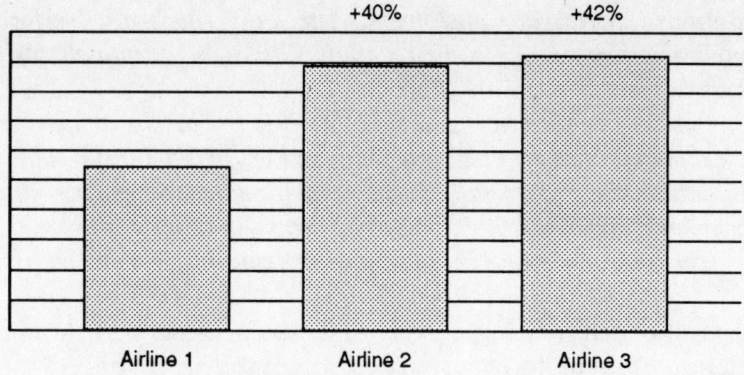

- Adjusted cycle reflects operative content.

- Airlines 2 and 3 show approximately the same productivity, while Airline 1 is much more productive

Figure 4.2   *Light Maintenance of Aircraft (Adjusted Cycle).*

Assuming that absolute comparability has been achieved, we can then compare quality and/or productivity. In the present case the comparison was between two traditional European airlines (2 and 3) with a background as monopoly national flag carriers, and a small, young but fairly well-established airline (1) that had grown up in a competitive climate. Figure 4.2 shows how they compared on productivity: all three were seen as equal with regard to quality of workmanship.

The newly started airline had succeeded in performing light maintenance about 80% more productively than its older-established counterparts by working in parallel, optimizing the flow of work and sharing tasks among the maintenance crew. An observation concerning this study, which is also generally applicable, is that the way a given job is performed differs not only among companies in the same industry but among local branches of the same company. In the present case, light maintenance was defined in different ways at different stations of the same airline.

Another example that produced striking results is taken from the telecom industry:

A traditional European telecom operator in an environment shielded from competition looked for reference points for its contracting operations for private customers. The unit concerned performed trouble-shooting as well as installation of lines and terminals for private households.

In this case the management did not want to confine the comparison to the telecommunications industry, which was felt to be tainted by a monopoly culture all over the world. So we found them a couple of other suitable benchmarks, one of which was a service company in the whiteware business. The comparison referred to trouble-shooting and installation.

As in all benchmarking exercises, it was necessary to standardize and eliminate to ensure true comparability. Standardization means making sure that the matched activities really are comparable, i.e. that they involve exactly the same operations and are measured in the same way. Elimination means cutting out anything that is not comparable.

As Figure 4.3 shows, the comparison revealed that productivity differed by a factor of five! The difference in productivity was found to be due to four main factors:

1   The telecom operator had manned its order switchboard with charm-school graduates, whereas the whiteware supplier had trained field repairmen answering the phone. As a result, they were able to do 30% of all their trouble-shooting

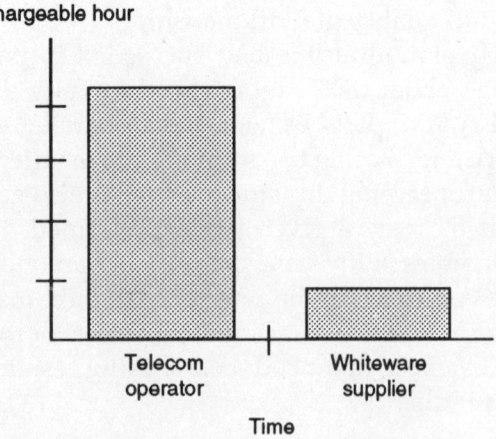

Figure 4.3   *Cost Per Work Order.*

by telephone: "Is the machine plugged in?" "Is the red but-
ton on the right-hand side in or out?" This way of doing
things carried its own reward for the repairmen, as it saved
them going out on wild-goose chases.

2   The telecom operator allowed customers a free choice of time
for service calls, while the whiteware supplier gave them
three options: "We can come tomorrow at eleven or nine
o'clock on Thursday or three o'clock on Friday afternoon.
Which would suit you best?" This difference in scheduling
accounted for a difference in productivity of as much as 20%.

3   The telecom operator had two divisional demarcation lines
to cross. The routines for these handovers were not op-
timized, which resulted in needless duplication of work and
discontinuities in the flow of activities.

4   In 1984 the whiteware supplier had reconstructed and op-
timized its information technology support to match its work
routines. The field repairmen, for example, were equipped
with mobitex communicators and could write out invoices
on the spot. The telecom operator had a patchwork of systems that did not communicate well with each other and
required a great deal of manual processing.

A QUESTION OF CONSCIENCE FOR LEADERS IN THE 1990s

The previous examples of benchmarking represent two distinct
types of case. In the first example the company compared itself
with a good example in the same industry, in this case civil aviation. That enabled the company to study how things were done
by the exemplary airline and to initiate a process of change that
was essentially in the nature of continual improvement, even
though the results in this particular case were quite striking.

The second example illustrates the possibility of using
benchmarking to achieve a breakthrough by comparing oneself
with a good example in an entirely different industry and thus
receiving an infusion of fresh thinking.

The quintessence of benchmarking is that it shifts the burden
of proof from the advocates of change to those who cling to the

status quo. Ordinarily, anyone who wants to make changes must be able to prove that they are necessary and beneficial. With benchmarking, the conservatives must show proof of why the change should not be made.

Both continual improvements and breakthroughs can be initiated on the basis of either possibilities that you have discovered yourself by using available methods or demands from outside which can at times be quite peremptory. It is therefore necessary to set up a signalling system to indicate when opportunities for improving efficiency arise. There is an inherent danger in running an enterprise by the traditional budgeting method. In the first place this tends to make the cost mass expand at the same rate as revenues – or worse, even faster. In the second place the growth of organizational bureaucracy, together with the increasing amount of energy consumed by internal friction, tends to obscure the existence of unproductive work, duplication of effort, discontinuities in the flow, etc.

In the 1990s every executive, regardless of the degree or kind of his or her responsibility, will have to answer the question: "How do you know that your operation is efficient?" This will compel and encourage leaders to do more about establishing criteria of efficiency in the dual sense of productivity and creation of value.

This is the principal explanation for the emergence of a series of new methods and approaches for giving leaders adequate early warning. The methods in question include:

- Total quality management (TQM)
- Goal-managed groups
- Benchmarking
- Business process re-engineering (BPR)
- Time-based competition
- Lean production

ZERO-BASE PLANNING

The specific purpose of this new set of methods is to monitor efficiency and to supply impulses for action. This applies both to

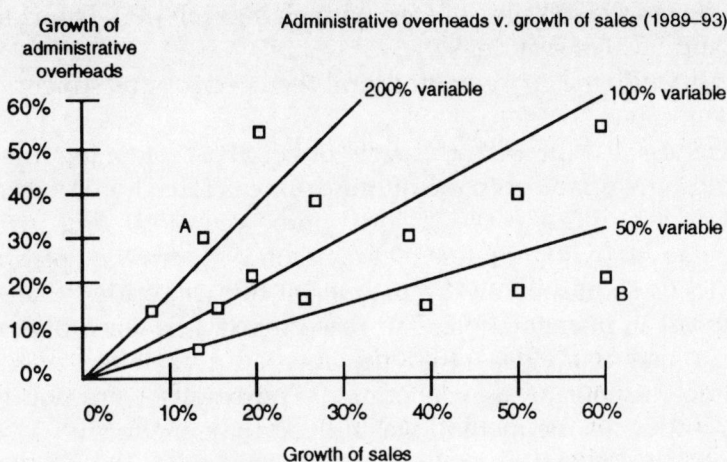

Figure 4.4 *Zero-base Planning.*

continual improvement and to openings for breakthroughs. My intention here is not to describe all the methods that exist to give an early warning of change. I would, however, like to mention briefly one more method which, unfortunately, has partly fallen into disrepute. This method was developed under the Carter administration in America and is called zero-base budgeting or zero-base planning. Its purpose was, and is, to take a radically critical view of all costs incurred, resources consumed and activities performed.

Figure 4.4 shows that Company A's administrative overhead costs had grown much faster than its sales, whereas the situation in Company B was the reverse. The 200% and 50% lines indicate cases where overhead costs grow two and a half times as fast as the volume of sales.

The procedure in zero-base planning is as follows:

1   Break down every function and process into activities for which specific goals can be defined in terms of efficiency.
2   Consider the consequences of dropping each specified activity altogether.
3   Work out alternative routines for performing each activity with a higher or lower level of service.
4   Calculate the costs and utility effects (quality) of each level of service.

5   Assess the risks associated with changes in the organization and level of service.
6   Quantify the consequences and the need for investment.

There are two important aspects of zero-base planning: first, it encourages a radical frame of mind. One is forced or induced to call one's present behaviour into question and assess alternatives in quantitative terms. Second, in zero-base planning the focus should be on the manner of thinking rather than the physical implementation. The reason why zero-base planning got a bad name was that the method was taken over by technocrats posing as economists. The results were not very impressive, so the method was judged to be ineffective. Just as value analysis was embraced by engineers in the manufacturing industry and the cost-benefit method by sociologists (often with left political leanings), so the zero-base approach has been "technocratized" by techno-economists.

Thus, the mind-set created by the zero-base approach is its most important component. As a leader, you free yourself from a load of preconceptions that would otherwise limit your ability to discover radically different solutions. If we study a situation in which a solution already exists, we tend to accept that solution. If we look instead at the problem to be solved and seek the best possible solution without prejudice, the potential for improvement will be much greater.

Make-or-buy analysis and BPR are both akin to zero-base planning. These distantly related concepts are mentioned in only passing here, as they are dealt with elsewhere in this book.

To conclude I want to emphasize that both continual improvement and breakthrough require willingness to change, willingness to learn and problem-solving ability. Power-oriented people and systems, as well as relation-oriented leaders who put relations with other people before efficiency (often found in the tax-financed public sector), often shy away from systematic comparisons with good examples. The balance between the constant search for ways to make small improvements in efficiency on the one hand, and radical changes based on zero-base thinking and creativity on the other, thus reflect another pair of opposite poles in the universe of leadership.

CONTINUAL IMPROVEMENT V. BREAKTHROUGH IMPROVEMENT IN RELATION TO THE COCE MODEL

As far as *customers* are concerned, the balance between this conflictual pair can be exemplified by model development in the automotive industry. Through the latter half of the 1980s and up to 1992, Volvo lived on its 700/900 series, then ten years old, and the 200 series with its roots in the 1960s. Customers were bored because the company had concentrated exclusively on continual improvement for far too long. The breakthrough came with the launch of the 800 series in 1992 which attracted wide attention and has since won Volvo several awards. Improvements from the customer's viewpoint can take the form of both better quality and lower prices, i.e. both axes of the Value Graph (see Figure 2.2).

Owners' desire for improvement is often unarticulated. They frequently develop an unexpressed dissatisfaction with the progress of change in a company or organization. The signal suddenly grows so strong that a chief executive is forced to resign or a trade union leader voted out of office, apparently without warning. The more institutionalized the ownership is, the weaker the system of signals. It is for this reason that the pace of innovation is so sluggish in banks, insurance companies and other institutionally owned organizations. It proves the importance of setting up a signalling system to detect and thereby articulate the owners' desire for improvements.

Costs often receive far too much of the "continual improvement" treatment, i.e. small incremental improvements in productivity. Sometimes, as a result, a company is caught unawares. This happened to Rank Xerox at the end of the 1970s when the Japanese launched much cheaper office copiers, and is now happening to a number of European airlines. Sometimes continual improvement is totally inadequate on the cost side. Benchmarking needs to be applied to well-chosen points of reference.

There are few areas in the world of organizations where *employees* can contribute so much as in that of improvement. People in the organization often sense a need for change in certain areas. This is not the case, however, in situations where a dogma of infallibility prevails, as it did to some extent at IBM. Hubris and belief in infallibility are the worst enemies of change management. Sometimes employees need to be put through benchmarking exercises to show them how the same kind of work is done in a completely different environment, and to force them to change their perspective and behaviour.

Try this exercise:

Start by making a list of the most important breakthroughs in your industry in the past ten years. By this I mean quantum improvements that gave their originators a substantial competitive edge for some time thereafter.

Then list the areas where you think it might be possible to look for radically new solutions leading to future breakthrough improvements. Are there any good examples that could be used as sources of inspiration?

Which three areas ought to be the prime candidates for continual improvement? To what extent are you already applying continual improvement in those areas?

5
Fact Base v. Judgement

There is an exceptionally tricky balance in the field of leadership which is best illustrated by the thesis of fact base and quantification and the antithesis of action based on judgement.

American leadership has a long-standing quantitative tradition with its roots in the theories of Adam Smith, the eighteenth-century economist, and F. W. Taylor, the father of division of labour and specialization. This tradition was carried on by Alfred Sloan, President and Chairman of General Motors from 1923 to 1956, and Robert MacNamara, President of Ford during the 1950s and Secretary of Defense in the Kennedy and Johnson administrations.

Adam Smith wrote the *Wealth of Nations* in 1776. Smith, a philosopher as well as an economist, recognized the opportunities that the Industrial Revolution offered for specialization of labour and automation. Through the use of such methods, the cost of producing an article could be reduced not just in small gradual steps but radically. The object was no longer to make labourers work faster, but to switch from manual labour to mass production.

Smith put his theories into practice in his famous pin factory, where he multiplied production capacity by having each worker perform only one operation. One worker drew the wire, a second straightened it, a third cut it, a fourth sharpened the points, a fifth ground the other end to take the head, and so on. Specialization and automation led to a hundredfold increase in productivity.

Most companies today still operate according to the same principle. The consequence of specialization is that work is fragmented: the larger an organization is, the smaller the pieces into which its work is fragmented. The method was refined at the turn of the century by F. W. Taylor, and the Experience Curve was developed to explain the increase in productivity that resulted from specialization of labour.

Operative management skills were developed during the nineteenth century. The growth of the railroad network in the United States not only accelerated economic development but also generated new knowledge of how to manage industrial systems. Railroad companies running trains on single-track lines had to develop standards and procedures to permit two-way traffic without the risk of collisions. Rules were written to cover every eventuality, and responsibility and authority were precisely defined, as were chains of command and reporting routines.

One might say that the companies were bureaucratized, or programmed. The aim was to make people do their work in a strictly regulated way to avoid the risk of making mistakes that might have disastrous consequences. The control systems that have been built up in many large corporations today have their origins in this principle of organization.

Henry Ford and Alfred Sloan refined the concept still further by bringing the work to the workers. Ford's invention of the endless belt was a breakthrough not only in the automotive industry. Elsewhere work was broken down into a number of simple manual operations.

The drawback of this principle was the difficulty of coordinating the people who were supposed to do the work. When Alfred Sloan succeeded William Durant as CEO of General Motors in 1923, he discovered that the company was finding it hard to adjust its production of various models to meet the demands of the market. He made management more efficient by setting up smaller, decentralized and more manageable divisions. This proved to be the ideal system for mass production. Sloan instituted one division per model series – Chevrolet, Cadillac, Oldsmobile, etc.

Alfred Sloan also applied the principle of division of labour to management. The top executives of GM were not required to have specialist knowledge of the automotive industry; what was needed instead was a knowledge of accounting and the requirements for control of operations via figures for profitability, capital commitment, order inflow, market share and sales volume. Alfred Sloan probably saved GM from extinction at a time when the Model T Ford was sweeping the US market. It was he who formulated GM's mission of making "a car for every taste and every pocket-book".

JUDGEMENT INSTEAD OF FIGURE ANALYSIS

Management by control of figures reached its zenith under chief executives like Harold Geneen at ITT and Robert MacNamara at Ford in the 1950s. Through detailed planning, top management was required to make forecasts of alternative scenarios and choose a course of action. This would enable resources to be deployed in areas where the prospects of success appeared the greatest.

This worked quite well up to the end of the 1960s due to a constant demand for goods and services throughout the world. Any refrigerator or any car was better than none at all. The present-day world, however, calls for new thinking and new principles of organization. We live in a world in which creation of value and customers' needs are more important than productivity and unit costs. As a result, the narrow focus on numerical fact bases has fallen out of favour, and rightly so, because it was often accompanied by a lack of understanding of important factors like trade logic, competitors' behaviour, and so on. In many parts of the world, the pendulum swung away from the previous blind faith in Management by Numbers. From the late 1970s to the late 1980s there was a strong undercurrent of criticism of the quantitatively-oriented American management tradition.

Such criticism has come from Robert Hayes, Professor of Management of Technology at the Harvard Business School, who reacted strongly against America's loss of competitive power, relating it to the widespread management training which exists in the United States but not, for example, in Japan. The heavy quantitative bias of American management training, he claimed, led to a short-sighted view of business development; it meant that long-term, visionary investments were neglected in favour of short-term profit improvement.

The counterreaction to the quantitative school of management was expressed in a number of catch-phrases like "paralysis through analysis". The notion of successful behaviour in the field of management underwent a radical reappraisal during the 1980s. The new criteria for success were action, entrepreneurship and energy. We came to rely on judgement instead of on figure-based analysis of facts.

Questions of judgement are unstructurable which makes them awkward to handle in the context of leadership. Experience and intuition play an important part in the exercise of judgement. Experience (uncountable) is defined here as the ability to sort a number of experiences (countable), discard those which do not contribute to greater knowledge, and draw conclusions accordingly. It is possible, in theory, to conceive of experiences which do not teach anything, but such experiences are in fact meaningless. An experience must thus be a learning experience to be worthy of the name.

Intuition is also based on experience. Intuition is defined here as the ability to draw conclusions from numerous elements of knowledge without necessarily being able to give a logical, sequential account of how one arrived at a particular conclusion. The intuitive person draws upon treasures stored in the cerebral cortex and senses which course of action should be taken in a given situation. Thus, intuition grows with increasing age and experience. A feeling for what is a successful pattern of behaviour in a given situation is often decisive in business because people often lack the time or capacity to absorb all the facts that would be needed to justify a decison in logical terms. In a person's unending struggle to make optimum use of his or her time, resorting to a fact base must constantly be weighed against the time it takes to gather the necessary facts.

Indecisiveness sometimes hides behind fact-gathering. Such behaviour is not uncommon among irresolute political assemblies. Awkward questions are simply referred to yet another commission of inquiry. Sometimes, of course, this is quite justified because the available fact base is insufficient for a proper decision or because the timing is wrong, but the real reason, very often, is indecisiveness – or a realization that there is no parliamentary hope of getting the measure approved.

Management consultancy has long been shaped by the need to reach better decisions by asking sensible people their opinion of a particular question. The European consultancy tradition has thus become oriented towards enlisting the help of a "wise man or woman" to get things done, as opposed to the American tradition which leans towards fact-based approaches and methods. The difference is due to divergent leadership traditions; it also arises out of the entrepreneurial ideal of the 1980s.

THE FACT BASE REVIVED

There is a risk of getting the balance between fact base and judgement incorrect. I myself have seen many decisions that were based on faith and opinion even where it would have been quite feasible in terms of time and money to acquire a solid base of facts. This can put a whole organization and its members in jeopardy.

In other cases, available numerical data have been treated in a cavalier fashion that risks giving fact-based analysis a bad name. The material that underlaid the proposal to merge Volvo and Renault was one example: the figures quoted varied so wildly as to arouse grave suspicion in the minds of outsiders. The claimed synergy effects increased in proportion to the growth of opposition to the merger. The following is an illustrative example of sales volumes:

An exceptionally well-reputed firm of financial consultants assessed the companies' future sales volumes. About 75% of Renault's passenger car sales were in France, Italy and Spain – countries where the importation of Japanese cars is effectively limited to a level far below that in less protectionist countries like Sweden and Germany.

By agreement with Japan, car imports will be successively deregulated throughout the European Union, which will mean a loss of volume for Renault on the Italian, Spanish and French markets. The consultants's report assumed that Renault would be able to make up the shortfall with other sales, but did not specify where.

If this assumption is correct, it means that the present management of Renault's passenger car division has been guilty of negligence in failing to sell cars on markets where it could have done so.

The quantitative analyses ordered by top managements are often performed by young, inexperienced people who often make assumptions that are not supported by the facts. The analytical team should therefore include an experienced person who is able to scrutinize the material in detail and point out discrepancies. If such a person is not included in the team, the result could be disastrous which could further damage the sullied reputation of fact-based analysis.

TIME AND CONSENSUS REFINE DECISIONS

It takes a delicate symbiosis between judgement and experience, and fact-based analysis to refine decisions for the benefit of the enterprise. There are, however, other factors in the decision equation: time and consensus. If decisions could be made without regard to the time factor and without the need to persuade a number of people to agree with them, the situation would be much simpler than it usually is in reality.

Time is a non-renewable primary human resource. This truth is not universally accepted, even though it is specially evident to consultants who charge time-based fees. Many taxi-drivers, for example, complain about the unprofitability of fares to airports lying tens of miles outside city centres. They intuitively assume that productivity, and thus costs, depend on distance, though with modern Western-world wages this is true only to a limited extent. Time is a much more important factor to the taxi-driver, who does not appreciate the advantage of a high-speed run with relatively low fuel consumption. The time factor predominates only in city rush-hour traffic, where speeds can be limited to 20 mph or less.

The precision of a fact base and the depth of an analysis can often be related to the time available. This has been done in the following list which ranges from "sell everything that can be sold right now to survive next month" to strategic benchmarking for long-term deployment of resources.

Time available:

Methods available:

1   Acute crisis.

- Win breathing-space by refinancing
- Shut down parts of the business
- Make extreme offers to bring in more cash
- Cancel all long-term projects in R & D, marketing, etc.
- Cut wages and salaries
- Sell everything that can be sold

2   Short-term need for profit improvement.

- Consider measures above
- Organization analysis for level reduction
- Overall budget cuts ("scythe")
- Renegotiate purchases
- Activity-based costing (ABC) analysis
- Business process re-engineering (BPR)
- Make-or-buy analysis

3   Medium term, 8 months–2 years.

- Methods as above
- Benchmarking
- Experience Curve
- Zero-base budgeting
- Capital reduction
- Internal demand analysis
- Reassign duties
- Value analysis
- Marketing audit
- BPR
- Lean production

4 Long term (variable according to type of industry).	• Methods as above • Strategy revision • Competition analysis • Market served and economies of scale (new markets) • Customer-perceived value and wider scope of delivery (new products) • Possible acquisitions and/or divestments

A further area which complicates decision-making is the tradition of consensus which is particularly strong in some countries. The function of consensus is to minimize conflicts and ensure that decisions are effectively executed. This is much easier if everybody agrees with the decision.

Sociological research shows that the consensus tradition varies not only throughout the world but also within Europe. A dividing line runs through the Baltic, west of the Netherlands, between the Flemish and Walloon parts of Belgium, and out into the English Channel.

To the west of this line there is a marked tradition of consensus, of collective decision-making and a striving for unanimity. The traditional picture to the east of it is that of the all-knowing, all-seeing Chief who leads the organization to success. This phenomenon has been recognized only partly, despite the fact that the research findings of Geert Hofstede, head of the Institute of Research on Intercultural Co-operation (IRIC) in Arnhem, were published ten years ago. It is of practical value in some situations, for example, where a Finn is appointed managing director of a Norwegian subsidiary or an English person as head of a German company. Some cultures regard the search for consensus as a sign of weakness; people expect the boss to know what he or she wants and make his or her wishes crystal clear. In those cultures it is considered weak to be relaxed, reflective or hesitant, or to ask others for advice.

Scandinavian managers have problems in America where people expect a more authoritative style of leadership than is customary in Scandinavia. Germans respond better than many others to brusque commands when something must be done with speed and precision. (This is a general observation which does not necessarily apply on the individual level.) Generalizations are useful and relevant, but, again, they should be applied with great caution.

GETTING THE SUMS WRONG

It is nearly impossible to consider the question of fact base v. judgement without including the degree of precision of forecasts which is often influenced by wishful thinking or sheer self-deception. How far this is intentional is difficult to tell, but it is quite obvious that many ventures would never have been undertaken if a correct fact base had been available.

In France, in particular, a combination of circumstances has led to a number of grandiose and horrendously expensive projects based on faulty calculations. The supersonic Concorde is a classic example. A more recent one is the Eurotunnel between England and France, which has proved to be a world-class budget-buster. In May 1994 the Swedish business magazine *Affärsvärlden* published the following summary of an article which had appeared in *The Economist*:

Mad Cathedral and Tunnel Builders

When the City Fathers of Seville decided to build a cathedral at the beginning of the 15th century, they declared their intention to make it so big that "succeeding generations must think us mad".

But whereas the cathedral builders declared their folly in advance, the men behind the Channel tunnel discovered theirs only after the event.

The premise was that a Channel tunnel could be built at a predictable, acceptable cost in a predictable, acceptable time and yield a good profit. They were proved wrong on every count.

The original cost estimate came to just under 5 billion pounds. Now the bill looks like being at least 10 billion pounds.

The timetable has proved illusory. The official opening by Queen Elizabeth and President Mitterand on 6 May was the only fixed date in an elastic calendar full of unkept schedules. Passenger traffic, which was to have begun in the first half of 1993, now looks like getting under way in the autumn (of 1994) at the earliest.

The effect of these galloping cost overruns and postponed revenues has been that the Eurotunnel has needed a series of fresh capital injections, the most recent in May, to the fury of the original shareholders. It also seems likely that yet another round of financing will be needed before the turn of the century.

No doubt one day, at the beginning of the next century, the Eurotunnel will start to generate a steady flow of long-term profits and dividends. But unfortunately for the original investors, it is the latecomer shareholders who will get the biggest payoff.

The quote illustrates two of the leadership conflicts discussed previously: facts v. judgement, and short term v. long term. Many monuments that now exist would never have been constructed if their builders had known in advance how much time and money it would take to complete the project or how long it would take for the project to be paid off.

OSTENSIBLE CONSENSUS

Ostensible consensus is a situation in which people nod agreement, vote with the majority and appear to support a project enthusiastically without actually sharing the prevalent opinion. The phenomenon is rife on all levels of Swedish society with its tradition of leadership and fear of open conflict.

The classic movie *12 Angry Men* offers a splendid example of how heavy group pressure is exerted to persuade a single dissenting juror to vote for the apparently obvious verdict of guilty. The film portrays one person's moral courage and ability to gradually sow seeds of doubt in the minds of the other jurors so that they eventually change their minds.

Ostensible consensus may have been present when Jan Carlzon, the visionary CEO of Scandinavian Airlines System (SAS), announced the purchase of shares in the Intercontinental Hotels chain, and probably also when SAS decided to launch a travel service chain for business travellers. The formal decision by the Volvo Board to merge with Renault was a clear-cut case. Subsequent events proved that many members of the Board did not vote according to their personal convictions but followed the Chairman's lead. Despite the enormous implications of the proposal for Volvo, the directors had evidently not studied the proposal in sufficient depth to be able to make well-founded individual judgements. This applies to several directors, and its truth was confirmed by the re-election of Sören Mannheimer to a seat on the Volvo Board despite the fact that the Group had adopted a policy diametrically opposed to the one he had voted for a few months earlier. The ability to change one's mind is a good thing and a sign of human greatness, provided that the person concerned possesses enough information to hold a fact-based opinion on both decision-making occasions.

DISCUSSION OF FACTS V. JUDGEMENT

Facts, judgement, the time factor and consensus all exert strong influence in a decision-making situation. As discussed in Chapter 2 on value and productivity, knowledge of value theory and fact-based approaches to the value side are often in short supply. This is due to the fact that the value axis of the Efficiency Graph is based on values which are subjective. There are two steps that one can take to avoid abandoning the attempt to put customer-perceived value on a factual basis:

1 Make a value analysis reflecting the customer's relative assessment of different components of value and his or her willingness to pay for them.
2 Identify points of measurement that give the best approximation of customers' value judgements.

Many failures in product launches could have been avoided if management, in certain situations, had attempted to make fact-based analyses of customer-perceived value. Value is defined here as a function of utility and price. Well-developed methods of handling productivity issues are available to management, and market analysis offers methods of handling quality. Value involves juggling with a combination of customer utility (quality) and productivity, i.e. determining the acceptable cost of a given utility.

Karlöf & Partners recently ran a project for a company that provides aftermarket service for machinery under contract. Their service contracts were written in such a way that the cost was related to the capital value of the equipment, which customers did not regard as relevant.

The company commissioned us to make an analysis of what factors customers would be willing to pay for and how much: response time, downtime, time needed for repairs, on-the-spot v. remote troubleshooting, etc. This analysis led to the formulation of a service contract that better matched customers' perceptions of value for their money.

The balance between fact base and judgement, together with time and consensus, is an important aspect of leadership. Figure 5.1 illustrates the relationship between the four components in decision-making. Here the factors are arranged in a four-field matrix so that the following discussion can focus on the intersections between them:

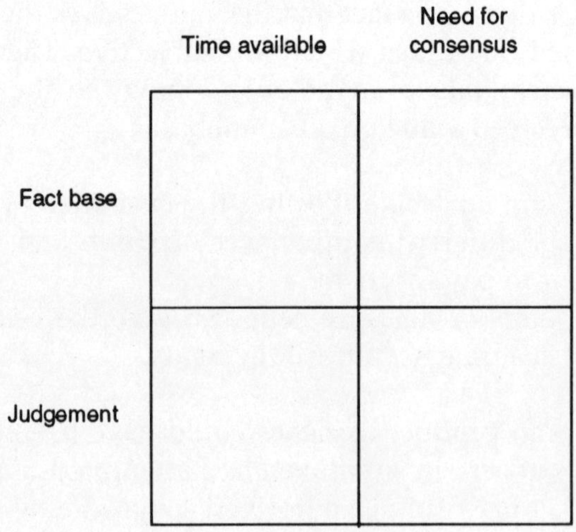

Figure 5.1   *Discussion of Facts v. Judgement.*

The relationship between fact base and time depends on the time available and the importance of the decision to the enterprise. Major decisions that must be made quickly call for a massive input of resources to compile a body of factual information. Judgement plays a bigger part when the decision must be made quickly than when there is plenty of time. There is a risk of trying to avoid making the decision by insisting on having more facts. This may be prompted by worry about the consequences of a bad decision or by general indecisiveness.

The relationship between fact base and consensus is a central yet oft-neglected issue. In our experience there is no better way to reach a consensus, thereby opening the gate from thought to action, than to present a correct and credible fact base. Thus, instead of trying to persuade and convince by arguing from judgement, you should put more effort into offering accepted and in-controvertible facts as a basis for consensus. Do not forget that the prime function of consensus is to aid implementation. By using correct fact bases you achieve two aims: you reach consensus more easily, and you smooth the way from discussion to decisive action.

The relationship between judgement and time can be viewed from two perspectives. Shortage of time may prevent you from doing a thorough job on the fact base, so, on the one hand, you will have to put greater trust in your experience and judgement. On the other hand, unfortunately, people put too much trust in their own judgement even when they have time to research facts. Many strong and highly successful leaders pin their faith on judgement even though they have both the time and the re-sources to develop a facts base.

The relationship between judgement and consensus can likewise be related to the behaviour of strong leaders, and to the pre-vious discussion about ostensible consensus. I know of a con-sultant firm whose charismatic senior partner was a very good consultant specializing in process consultancy, i.e. in finding solutions to organizational problems and getting people to agree to problem descriptions. This excellent consultant gradually developed the ambition to run his firm as a conglomerate with a combination of structural growth and diversification. By virtue of his acknowledged skill and his position in the company he persuaded the other partners to accept his proposals. Growth eventually led to dubious property deals abroad and the acquisition of financial businesses, and ultimately to spectacular failures. The moral of the story is that skill and good judgement in one field are not always transferable to other fields.

Scandinavian Airlines System's ambitions to expand its scope of delivery to include ground transport, hotel accommodation, etc. were likewise accepted under the pressure of a charismatic personality, a strong position of power and documented good judgement in previous ventures having to do with value creation. A fact base was not developed until afterwards, when the project had already proved to be misguided.

FACT BASE V. JUDGEMENT IN RELATION TO THE COCE MODEL

Fact-based analysis is applied much less frequently in relation to *customers* than to, say, costs and capital. The fact base is harder to compile because we are often dealing with subjective perceptions and subtleties. However, the sum of a number of subjective perceptions represents a fact-based objective truth.

Judgement based on intuition is used too much in relation to customers. I have seen many new product configuration projects launched without reference to a fact base. This is difficult to achieve, but can be very rewarding.

Owners are too often inclined to trust their judgement and that of the company's management. The management almost invariably holds a great advantage in terms of information, which makes it difficult for owners' representatives on the Board to form an independent opinion. Institutional owners often neglect to acquire their own independent picture of the facts, finding it less troublesome to assume that the management knows what it is doing.

Costs are the easiest element to factualize. Systematic comparisons can be made according to the following important frames of reference:

- Developments over a period of time
- Zero-base budgeting
- Systematic comparison with good examples

In the last-named case it is essential that the examples are relevant and not chosen just because they are the most accessible.

Employees were poorly schooled in fact-based decision-making during the flamboyant boom years of the 1980s. Many companies and organizations would have done well to adopt a more fact-base-oriented cultural pattern that would have improved the precision of their decisions. Jack Smith, now CEO of General Motors (GM), always asked his subordinates the same question when he was head of GM in Europe: "Have you benchmarked?" That question was an expression of a demand for fact-based decision-making with the right standard of comparison.

Try this exercise:

Review the history of your enterprise and search for decisions where the fact base was less complete than it could have been.

Are there any areas in your enterprise where judgement is neglected in favour of exaggerated analysis? Are there any examples in your organization of ostensible consensus, i.e. of signified agreement unsupported by genuine unanimity?

What does the balance between fact base and judgement look like in your corporate culture? Could it be better?

6
Organic Growth v. Structural Growth

During the late 1980s a well-known executive of a large company specializing in office supplies was interviewed by a Swedish business magazine. The essence of what he said was that the group had no time to grow organically but had to grow by acquisition. Several companies were acquired at very high prices. Those companies were "structured" to fit the corporate pattern, with the result that the entrepreneurial spirit was suffocated and their performance was much poorer than it had been when they were independent.

That executive's pronouncement is symptomatic of a heavily power-oriented frame of mind. Power-oriented people often fail to grasp the true criteria of successful businessmanship. Growth through financial clout alone is hardly ever successful. Many corporations, including General Motors, Volvo and Daimler-Benz, have discovered this the hard way. Success can only be achieved with a feeling for trade logic, business acumen and ability to compete, i.e. to deliver good value to customers with high productivity.

The fundamental requirements for organic growth are:

1 Development of products (goods and services) that offer customers good value (quality in relation to price).
2 Skill in communicating the offering to prospective customers (marketing) and winning orders (selling).

3   Rational production of the offering of goods and services (productivity).
4   Administration of the enterprise at the lowest cost that can be managed without jeopardizing any of the other functions.

These four factors – development, marketing, production and administration – are the basic functions of all organized activity. A deft touch on this keyboard makes the company's products attractive, enlarges its market share and improves the look of its bottom line. Organic growth is the hallmark of true enterprise and of accomplishing what one sets out to do. Success in enterprise provides a foundation for all other ventures, including acquisition of companies.

Structural growth involves acquisition, amalgamation and sometimes divestment of whole business units or parts thereof. Acquisitions may be synergetic or may lead to diversification. Figure 6.1 illustrates types of growth.

As a general observation, we note that the difficulties inherent in structural growth are invariably underestimated by the acquiring party. The seller often feels he or she has been paid a good price, while the buyer can seldom get his or her cost accounting anywhere near the cost estimates made before the acquisition.

Organic growth with a structural component occurs when a genuine merger takes place; this is a fairly rare event. A genuine merger is the result of realization by two parties that they can grow stronger by joining forces and that real synergy exists, i.e. that the profits, market shares or success of the combination will be greater than the sum of the success of the two enterprises operating independently. One of the stumbling-blocks of the

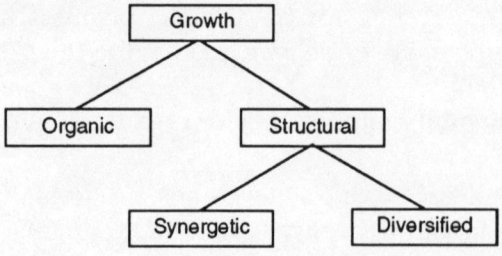

Figure 6.1   *Types of Growth.*

proposed merger between Renault and Volvo was that Volvo regarded the amalgamation as a true merger, whereas Renault and the French Establishment viewed it as an acquisition. Although the actual difference between the two is often negligible, the psychological difference is great. Being acquired tends to be regarded as a capitulation and, thus, as a mark of failure.

One factor which explains the success of organic growth over structural growth is that the advance is made incrementally. Development is a process of trial and error: you have time to correct mistakes as you go along, without the risk of major disasters. This applies in most cases though there are exceptions, such as when an automotive company builds a car that nobody will buy, or a new wonder drug turns out to have horrible side effects. The pharmaceutical industry offers the following classic examples, both Swedish, of companies characterized by organic and structural growth respectively:

Astra, now reaping the fruits of its success with the ulcer medicine Losec, predicted to become the world's best-selling pharmaceutical, is living proof of the benefits of growing organically and sticking strictly to core business. Since Astra's former managing director Ulf Widengren sold off a number of peripheral enterprises in the 1970s, the group has never let its well-filled coffers seduce it into either acquiring or diversifying. Almost all of Astra's products are the result of its own in-house research.

Pharmacia is Astra's opposite in most respects. The group in its present form is the result of no fewer than eight mergers over the past twenty years. Lacking new drugs of its own to sustain growth, Pharmacia has bought growth. Its profits are largely due to cost-cutting. Most of Pharmacia's principal products were developed by research institutes outside the group.

If we are going to discuss the pros and cons of organic and structural growth, we must be careful to distinguish the motives of the parties involved. These parties can be divided into three main categories:

- Owners
- Customers (industrial motives)
- Management

Owners' motives are generally based on a desire to enrich themselves – in monetary terms if the enterprise is a commercial one.
These motives may sometimes be totally incompatible with the
best interests of the enterprise. The following is an example from
my own experience:

The owner of a European company in an expansive industry regarded
himself as a poor man. Apart from a sizeable block of shares in the
company, he owned an ordinary mortgaged house, a car and some other
necessary minor chattels.

The company's business was doing well. The rapid growth of the
industry in which it operated, combined with competent management,
had helped it grow to a point at which it attracted a takeover bid from
an American company in the same industry. Accepting the offer would
neatly solve the owner's financial problems. He therefore began to
search for industrial motives for the takeover.

My company, in our capacity as advisers, conducted some reviews to
analyse the situation. We distinguished the owner's motives from the
industrial motives. Both aspects were irreproachable as such, but
needed to be considered separately for analytical purposes. Incidentally,
the management adopted a neutral stance and offered no proposal of its
own, which is unusual in such cases.

After careful review we found that the owner's motives and the
industrial motives had been intermingled, and recommended that these
issues ought to be, and could be, resolved separately. The result was
that the company declined the offer, while the owner's problem was
solved by selling shares to a couple of institutions. Our doubts about
the industrial prospects for success were largely prompted by an analy-
sis of what would probably happen to production, marketing and
product development, and our misgivings about the cultural problems
that would probably arise in the event of a merger with an American
company.

Since then the quoted share price of that company has almost trebled
as a result of enlarged sales volume and internal improvements.

There are a number of external factors which influence companies towards diversifying instead of letting their shareholders
do so. Aside from the empire-building motives of management,
the European tax system exerts powerful lock-in effects in that

the State takes a substantial percentage if profits are distributed to the owners. These fiscal considerations are so strong in many countries that returning the owners' stakes is not a feasible option. Taxes on dividends are much higher than taxes on corporate profits. This prompts managements to use the capital generated by their core business for outward investment, either in real estate or in other unrelated enterprises.

The power orientation of management is a central motive for structural growth. A power-oriented person is one who puts his or her own advantage before that of the enterprise. Performance-oriented people, on the other hand, get their satisfaction from seeing the enterprise grow and prosper.

Another motive is management's need to keep itself occupied. If everything is going smoothly, there is no real need for management. Whereas adversity and setbacks keep managements occupied full-time, prosperity leaves them with time on their hands. The natural thing would then be to channel the energy of management into organic growth, but it is by no means certain that the managements of large corporations have the aptitude or inclination for that. In these career-ladder-climbing days the managements of big corporations often consist of people who do not know the trade logic of their own business well enough to take organic initiatives. In prosperous times when the business is running itself, managements are apt to turn their attention to acquisitions and structural growth.

The motives that corporate executives cite for acquiring companies often bring smiles to the faces of people who really know the industry concerned. There are few areas where imagination is given such free rein or where excursions into the shadowlands of truth are so blatant as in the justification of structural growth. The world is full of imaginary synergies.

There are a number of aspects of synergy that can provide an analytical framework in the context of structural growth:

1 Shared resources, e.g. common functions such as sales force, R & D and purchasing.
2 Transfer of know-how between amalgamated units.
3 Transferable similarities in trade logic and corporate culture, e.g. between soft drinks and cigarettes.

4   Added value to customers in the form of combined offerings, e.g. air travel and hotel accommodation or consultant firms offering a range of specialities.
5   Shared image, which enhances the status of some business units through identification with others of high repute.

SUCCESS CANNOT BE BOUGHT

An intellectual trap into which even well-managed companies often fall is to confuse the causes of the Experience Curve with its effects. There is a proven correlation between high market share and high profitability. That correlation was demonstrated in the mid-1920s by the commanding officer of the Wright Patterson Base, the USAF R & D facility. The logic is that:

1   The Experience Curve shows that cost advantages increase with the accumulated volume of production.
2   Prices fall with time at a predictable rate.
3   A high market share is desirable because it provides a large volume of accumulated production, and thus experience.
4   If the cost advantages of the Experience Curve are utilized, high production volumes will give high margins.
5   The high margins can be utilized either to erect a price umbrella, thereby securing profitability that is greater than the industry average, or to cut prices, capture additional market shares and perhaps even force competitors out of the market.

Structural measures such as acquisitions are often justified by the claim that they boost market shares and thereby profits. This cause-and-effect relation, however, is open to question. You win a large market share by earning it, i.e. by delivering products of high value to customers with low production costs. You cannot automatically conclude that buying another company in the industry will give you the same advantages that you get from organic growth.

There are differences between the effects of the Experience Curve on costs and revenues. These can be summarized as follows:

1 The price side of the Experience Curve is governed by market dynamics and competition.
2 The cost side, on the other hand, is a management responsibility.
3 Utilizing the Experience Curve does not guarantee quality. Quality may actually deteriorate when costs go down.
4 Sudden substitutions or technological innovations can break the Experience Curve. Such discontinuities need to be identified, as competitive advantage may otherwise be lost.
5 The Experience Curve can be applied to service-providing companies; the degree of applicability increases with the degree of repetitiveness involved in the service they provide.
6 Drawing Experience Curves for individual functions within an enterprise reveals what variables influence the shape of the curve.
7 The competitor with the greatest accumulated experience has the potential to earn the highest margins.

A leader's ability to apply the effects of the Experience Curve to productivity is a crucial skill in organization development. As we pointed out in Chapter 2, it cannot be taken for granted that the same individual is capable of dealing with both axes of the Efficiency Graph.

The pros and cons of large-scale and small-scale operation are an integral part of the general discussion of the economies of scale. If economies of scale could be extrapolated to infinity, or if the curve were asymptotic, there would only be one company in each industry. The companies that managed the Experience Curve best would be assured of a permanent productivity advantage and could thus systematically out-compete their rivals out of existence. This does not happen in real life because there are other factors that act as a counterbalance. These factors will be discussed in Chapter 7.

ORGANIC GROWTH SOWS THE SEED OF STRUCTURAL GROWTH

Many business executives have never previously started, run or been responsible for a company or a business unit. A business unit is defined here not by its formal organizational structure (limited company, division, etc.), but by the four elements of corporate mission. They are as follows:

- Needs and demand
- Customers and distributors
- Offering of goods and services
- Competitive advantage

The value created in a business enterprise almost always proceeds from the business skills of a management that pursues organic growth. There are occasional exceptions to this rule in cases where financial skill generates values that remain unidentified.

To simplify, we can say that organic growth is an expression of skill in business, whereas structural growth is more often a product of financial skills. Aside from the empire-building urge and the lock-in effects of the taxation system, structural ambitions may be inspired, for example, by a surplus of cash and resources. Skilful organization development may generate high liquidity which cannot be distributed as dividends on account of the tax system. Instead, financially oriented parties take command and pursue structural growth instead of organic growth.

The Volvo Car Corporation was in serious trouble in 1975 and 1976. The President-elect, Håkan Frisinger, worked hard at solving quality problems and developing a new model. This new model was launched in 1982, by which time the company was out of its difficulties. Håkan Frisinger's subsequent resignation was followed by a harvest-time, with enormous profits by the standards of those days.

The surplus was only partly invested in organic growth; most of it was used for structural ventures including the purchase of part of Renault. The next model therefore took a long time and a lot of money to develop. Competitors like BMW took the opportunity to make great gains at Volvo's expense.

In other words, organic growth sows the seed of structural growth, and the loss of focus on development of the products and markets that constituted the substrate for organic growth.

This phenomenon is caused by prosperity, hubris and spare cash crying out to be profitably spent. Thus, successful management and organic growth often lead to executives being promoted to a higher division where they become portfolio managers striving for structural growth. The difference, however, between a business manager and a portfolio manager is one of kind, not of degree.

RISK-SPREADING: AN ILLUSORY MOTIVE

Risk-spreading is a frequently cited motive for structural manipulation, as in Volvo's example. All experience indicates, however, that risk-spreading is a difficult art, for several reasons. If your declared intention is to spread your risk, you have implicitly acknowledged that some business units will be suboptimally managed in hard times. That, in turn, can lead to complaisance, laxity and an administrative attitude marked by lack of dynamism. Concentration on business enterprises without risk-spreading puts the management under pressure to do its utmost in any given situation to make the enterprise successful.

It has further been found that risk-spreading seldom produces the desired result. This is because business cycles run in phase regardless of type of industry. They do not, however, run in phase in different parts of the world. If you want to spread your risks within a given industry, you should consider acquisitions in Australia or New Zealand, for example, where business cycles are regularly two or three years out of phase with those in Europe. Even the United Kingdom is normally at a different point on the cycle compared to, say, France, Germany or Sweden.

Much of the contents of this chapter would be self-evident to someone reading it in the mid-1990s for we are currently in a wave of concentration on core business, make-or-buy analysis and divestment of peripheral activities. It is important to remember that this has not always been the case, and that the periods of diversification and concentration regularly succeed each other, just like business cycles and ice ages. You can be quite sure that a boom period, reinforced by the lock-in effects of the tax system, will spark off a fresh period of structural flamboyance. This chapter should therefore be read with a somewhat longer time frame in mind than that of the present day.

The following is an example from Eastman Kodak which illustrates the spirit of 1994:

George M. C. Fisher has made a number of major decisions in the short time since his appointment as President of Eastman Kodak Co. After only five months he announced the sell-off of three large units including Sterling Drug Inc., purchased for 5.1 billion dollars as recently as 1988. Thus at one blow Fisher has reversed the ill-starred strategy of diversification adopted by his predecessor which led to a heavily debt-laden balance sheet.

By doing so he has also declared his intention to concentrate on Kodak's core business, image reproduction. In that area he is pursuing an offensive strategy with a view to building a future based on new technologies like digital image reproduction and all-electronic cameras, thermal printers and electronic storage methods like photo-CDs.

In addition, Fisher has tackled some of the problems that the group has had in controlling its central operations. A highly complicated matrix organization had made it impossible to pin responsibility for profit development on any single manager. He has also decided to set up a digital image group to promote the new technologies independent of traditional photography.

He has further used benchmarking on an extensive scale and studied Kodak's trade logic in depth, unlike his predecessors who adhered to the American tradition of Management by Numbers.

CORE BUSINESS V. DIVERSIFICATION

Concentration on core business v. diversification and organic v. structural growth are two closely related pairs of opposites, but they are not mutually exclusive. Figure 6.2 illustrates a matrix of these four concepts. The organic growth/core business and structural growth/diversification fields in the matrix represent natural combinations and require no further comment.

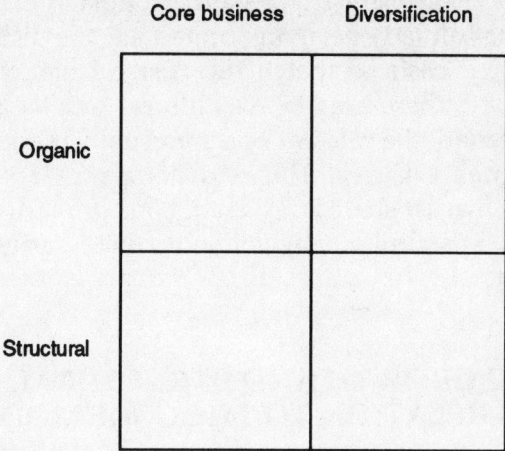

Core business   Diversification

Organic

Structural

Figure 6.2 *Organic and Structural Growth in Relation to Core Business and Diversification.*

Organic growth would appear to have little in common with diversification, or structural growth with core business, but organic growth can be combined with diversification, e.g. in situations where a technology developed in one industry opens up a market in an entirely different industry. Here it is the technology that provides the organic unity. The DOPPIN feeders developed at the Volvo Car Corporation Olofström Plants are a good example:

The DOPPIN Feeder was originally developed to solve an in-house problem in the Olofström Plants, where most of the body panels for Volvo Cars are pressed. The need to transfer sheet metal blanks and stampings between presses at high speed, with high precision and without damage, was met by an ingenious mechanical linkage system equipped with suction-cup grippers. This system was patented, and subsequently led to the establishment of Olofström Engineering as a supplier of automation equipment to the automotive industry at large. This organic diversification was made possible by the strong financial position of the Volvo Group during the 1980s combined with the relative autonomy enjoyed by the Olofström Plants.

Structural development of a core business is easier to understand; it consists simply in making acquisitions which complement or supplement the basic product. A classic pitfall in such cases has already been mentioned, i.e. the difficulty of getting the actual costs to match the cost calculations made beforehand. First, there are always cultural problems to contend with, and second, the calculations are usually made on the basis of the Experience Curve. This is a dangerous assumption because a high market share is advantageous primarily when it has been earned by skilful management, not necessarily when it has been bought.

ORGANIC GROWTH AND STRUCTURAL GROWTH IN RELATION TO THE COCE MODEL

Customers often push organic growth. Wrong analyses of customers' needs may lead to erroneous and mistimed conceptions of customers' needs, e.g. combinations of telecommunications and computers or of hotels and air travel. Organic growth often enhances value to customers, while structural growth is not infrequently prompted by the empire-building ambitions of management. The latter can result in irrelevant and unwanted offerings to customers.

Owners frequently find that structural growth yields poorer dividends than organic growth, especially if it takes the form of diversification. Conglomerates seldom if ever give a sustained high return on investment. Owning a company that grows structurally is often more a matter of capital management than of whole-hearted commitment to a core business. The lock-in effects of the tax system, together with the ambitions of management, often result in structural rather than organic growth.

Companies and organizations that grow organically are often better at controlling their *costs* than those which grow in other ways. Misjudgements of synergies in structural growth abound, whether the structural growth is related to the core business or not. Surprisingly often, predicted cost savings from acquisitions and mergers fail to materialize.

The principal rule as far as *employees* are concerned is that cultural problems increase in proportion to the level of skill in companies and organizations. Trivial tasks tend more and more to be automated, with the results that the intelligence content of the remaining work rises. Employees thus become increasingly aware of the importance of their own performance and increasingly reluctant to accept foreign methods and processes. Cultural problems and employee motivation are becoming ever more important factors in the context of structural growth. Expansion does however reward one small group of employees – those in management – with higher pay and a sense of success.

Try this exercise:

What structural transactions has your organization made in the past ten years?

What organic growth has taken place in the past ten years? (The term "organic" is defined here by the criteria for a business unit – products, services, markets, etc. – given in this chapter.)

How do your structural and organic expansions appear now in the critical light of hindsight? What conclusions can you draw from them?

How do you define your core business and core skills?

7
Centralization v. Decentralization

For more than a decade, decentralization has been extolled and acclaimed as a sustaining and indisputable principle of leadership. The upward-pointing curves of the 1980s accelerated the drive to decentralize. Large corporations split into divisions and subsidiaries in the firm conviction that decentralization was a way to achieve greater efficiency in business. This conviction was based on the following propositions:

1 The growing importance of customer-perceived value makes it necessary to have receptors placed closer to customers than they used to be.
2 Large corporations can avoid the disadvantages of scale by breaking down their operations into smaller units.
3 More executives can be given a chance to exercise independent authority and develop business skills.

There are also a number of other, more individual-related motives. Some executives possess a genuine performance motivation and want their own platform where they can prove to themselves and the world at large that they are capable of running an enterprise with all its dimensions. Decentralization is regarded by many as a route to greater personal freedom and thus to professional success. In other cases more diffuse, status-related and power-oriented motives underlie the individual's desire for an area of personal authority. An unfortunate example is the computer software companies that split into large numbers of subsidiaries during the 1980s. These splits were often prompted by the desire of executives to style themselves as President or Managing Director.

The issue of centralized or decentralized decision-making is a very important one. Unbridled decentralization led to a number of calamities during the rapid and sometimes explosive expansion during the 1980s. The world of banking offers numerous shocking examples of irresponsible lending that resulted from uncritical and uncontrolled decentralization; local bank managers made loans for real estate purchases in other parts of the country or even abroad, projects whose viability they had no way of assessing.

A leader must be capable of judging the pros and cons of centralized or decentralized decision-making in a given situation. The input for decision-making consists of a large number of parameters, only a few of which are quantifiable. That is a good starting-point for understanding the rationale of decentralization. One approach is to mirror the advantages of large-scale operation which include:

1   Economies of scale – the distribution of high fixed costs over a large number of units produced.
2   The Experience Curve which shows that learning, changes in organization and automation lead to lower unit costs, i.e. higher productivity.
3   "Economies of skill" – the accumulation of a critical mass of skills in certain central areas.

The advantages of a large-scale operation have often been exaggerated. The curve that describes them is not only asymptotic (progressively flatter) but actually U-shaped; in other words, an advantage derived from a large-scale operation eventually becomes a disadvantage. The following example is taken from the automotive industry:

It has been received wisdom for the past two decades that the advantages of a large-scale operation in vehicle manufacturing are so vast that small manufacturers must necessarily be swallowed up by big ones to survive as marques or labour-employing industries. This argument applied, for example, to Ford's acquisition of Jaguar and General Motors' purchase of 50% of Saab Automobile. The planned merger of Volvo's automotive operations with the French Renault Group was based on the same idea.

The economies of scale in the automotive industry have shifted from production to product development and marketing. The fixed costs of building a company's trademark or the image of a model have come to exceed those of tooling, distribution, etc.

It is now increasingly claimed that virtual organizations, e.g. for joint development of components, are a fully adequate alternative to integration of companies. Such collaboration, in many cases, more than makes up for shortage of volume. Hardening competition and rising overproduction in the automotive industry have displaced the advantages of scale from production via development to marketing.

Available statistics show no evidence that large car factories are more profitable than small ones (see Figure 7.1).

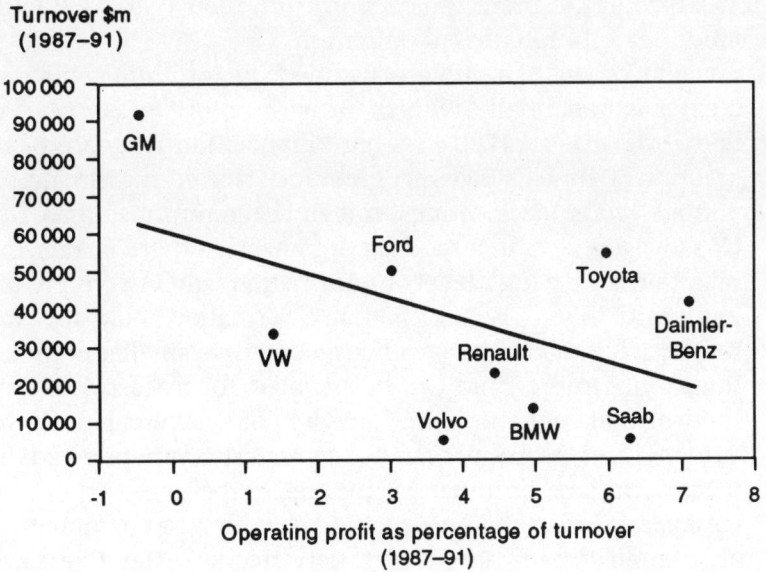

Figure 7.1 *Automotive Industry: Turnover and Profit.*

ADVANTAGES OF SMALL SCALE

The advantages of large scale diminish with increasing volume and eventually turn into disadvantages. The following are six possible explanations for why this occurs.

- Motivation and energy
- Communications
- Customer service
- Optimum processes
- Cost management
- Inflexibility of trade unions

1   *Motivation and energy.* One of the most important advantages of small scale is that people feel more motivated when they have an overview of a whole process, even if it is just part of a larger system. This causes them to put more of their vital energy into their work, which in turn leads to higher productivity and a generally greater commitment to the task in hand. This situation favours both employees and employers. The former get more satisfaction from their work, while the latter get a more efficient operation.

2   *Communications.* The time consumed by communications increases exponentially with the size of an organization. Anybody who has worked in a big organization is aware of the amount of time it takes to give and receive information of various kinds via meetings, travel, telecommunications, data transmission, etc. In a modern organization there is a need to maintain a very high level of information, and everybody in it has a duty to supply information. Information is like love and money; we can never have enough of it. In a smaller organization, much more time can be devoted to processes and activities that enhance productivity or customer-perceived value. This is probably one of the greatest competitive advantages of the small company compared to the large corporation.

3   *Customer service.* Closeness to and devotion to customers enable small organizations to satisfy needs better than large ones. The employees are directly exposed to movements on the value axis of the Efficiency Graph, and therefore give

more efficient service to customers, members, etc. Scandinavian Airlines System under Jan Carlzon's leadership pulled off a master-stroke in this respect in 1983, when decentralized decision-making led to a quantum jump in the quality of customer service.

4 *Optimum processes.* These processes and activities proceed from the need of a growing organization to break down its operations into ever-smaller portions, with the attendant risk of discontinuities in work flows. The whole of process thinking is based on a flow concept and on the need to eliminate expensive, time-consuming interruptions of the flow. The flows in a small organization are more easily manageable, and this benefits both productivity and customer-perceived value.

5 *Cost management.* Cost-consciousness tends to diminish as the size of an organization increases. In other words, large organizations contain a much larger element of a planned economy, where various operative units deliver goods and services to each other with no free choice of alternative suppliers. The organization becomes prone to an allocation mentality which erodes cost-consciousness.

6 *Inflexibility of trade unions.* Large companies have strong union branches which limit flexibility by drawing demarcation lines and thus preventing people from doing what needs to be done. The comprehensive Profit Impact of Marketing Strategy (PIMS) research database compiled in the United States, contains documented proof that company profitability diminishes with increasing degree of union organization. This database covers about 3,000 business units world-wide. A recent study of airline efficiency pointed to the same conclusion: larger airlines have lower productivity in certain operative functions because union membership puts constraints on who is allowed to do what. Please note that this is an analytical observation, not a general expression of hostility to the trade union movement.

MAKE OR BUY: CONCENTRATION ON CORE SKILLS

The question of whether to make or to buy is akin to the conflict between centralized organization and decentralized organization. This is an issue that every organization in Europe's highly integrated systems must sooner or later face. To be more efficient, the organization must decide what core skills it needs to concentrate on and what it should allow others to do. All types of enterprise will be subject to a review of what they do themselves and what they buy. This will lead to a healthy shift from planned-economy thinking to a more market-oriented approach.

The make-or-buy issue affects both the advantages of large scale in centralized operations and the advantages of small scale in decentralized ones. Large organizations conduct many operations in which the advantages of large scale do not apply. These may include everything from component manufacturing and office cleaning to high-level staff functions like strategy development.

Notions of self-sufficiency and a desire for a large organization with a large turnover often lead to irrational retention of in-house operations. The motive for buying a given article or service from an outside supplier is usually that it is a product of that supplier's particular core skill. This generally leads to more dynamic development and higher productivity because concentration in itself makes product development essential to survival. The supplier can also, by utilizing Experience Curve effects, achieve a lower unit cost which further contributes to productivity. The advantage of decentralization seen in this perspective is specialization of the economy inherent in long production runs.

The question of whether to buy things from outside the organization or to make them within is also highly relevant to the advantages of small scale. Greater motivation, better cost management, concentration on core business, simpler communications and the other aforementioned advantages of small scale all argue that it is more efficient to buy from an independent source.

Ultimately, however, it is the degree of freedom enjoyed by the buyer that is crucial to the promotion of efficiency. Fake commercialization is no use; turning one of a corporation's functions into a subsidiary company while still requiring the other functions to buy from that company is a pointless exercise.

Without the basic criterion of the buyer's freedom to choose, decentralization and similar measures have little effect.

The limit to how far it pays to buy from outside is set by transaction costs, as Nobel Laureate Ronald Coase has shown. If the transaction cost exceeds market-economy profit, it is better to keep the operation in-house. This principle is easier to understand in theory than to apply in practice, but it is nevertheless worthwhile to attempt the analysis.

ADVANTAGES OF LARGE SCALE AND SMALL SCALE: A DIFFICULT BALANCING ACT

The respective advantages of large- and small-scale operations are seldom analysed thoroughly. Many potential economies of scale go unutilized, while at the same time there is a lack of realization of where the advantages of small scale lie. Established expertise uses instruments like the Experience Curve for its analyses, whereas the science of business administration seldom concerns itself with the small-scale aspects, probably because the latter are harder to quantify and lie more in the field of behavioural sciences, e.g. motivation, customer service, resource management, and so on.

In my practice I have often encountered the paradox of vast unrealized economies of scale side-by-side with lack of appreciation of the advantages of small scale. National and regional politics have led to the erection of barrier structures which are quite unnecessary in this age of information technology. Scandinavian Airlines System's three-base set-up (one each in Denmark, Norway and Sweden) has cost enormous sums over a long period of time. Though its irrationality has been recognized, considerations of national prestige have prevented anything from being done about it – until now.

We find the same situation if we look at the network structures of telecom companies. The number of lines per switching point in all the Nordic countries is far below the corresponding key indicator for telecom operators in other parts of the world. Europe, as a whole, has similar problems. Each country has its own importer, agent, etc. for a given product, they cost a percentage of the product's price, and their only real function is that of cultural intermediary in their respective countries.

It is not easy to strike an optimum balance between the quantifiable advantages of large scale and the organizational and behavioural-science advantages of small scale. The leader must be capable of weighing the tangible against the intangible, just as he or she must be able to weigh quantifiable productivity against hard-to-measure value creation.

The book *The Multinational Mission*, written by C. K. Prahalad and Yves Doz, Professors of Strategy at the University of Michigan and INSEAD in France respectively, has inspired the creation of an analytical framework for such difficult comparisons. The following list of apparently simple questions offers a good guide to the division of responsibilities and methods of organization:

1 What advantages of scale exist in our industry/company?
2 What activities and processes are of such strategic importance as to require strict co-ordination?
3 What activities and processes lend themselves best to local adaptation?
4 In what parts of our operations can small-scale advantages be created on a basis of motivation, communication and customer-perceived value?
5 What areas require a central overview for control and supervision of operations?

DECENTRALIZATION PUTS LEADERS TO THE TEST

Operations in the tax-financed public sector and other enterprises in Europe that are cushioned against competition have sometimes been decentralized on a basis of territorial thinking, i.e. the desire of department heads for full authority over their little piece of the organization. In my business I have encountered European airlines and telecom operators that lack congruent accounting systems to control their operations. The harder the pressure of competition, the more important it is to strike the right balance between centralization and decentralization.

A harsh competitive climate or a business recession reveals how good the balance really is. Some companies and organizations have found it necessary to go in for strict centralization in order to regain profitability in hard times. Decentralized responsibility is fairly easy to handle when things are going smoothly and the curves are rising, but not so easy in periods of adversity and stiffening competition that involve mental stress and unpalatable decisions. The question of whether to centralize or decentralize ought not to be unduly influenced by the current situation or state of the market, which means that it requires very careful thought.

A decentralized organizational structure makes different demands on managers – the same demands are similar to those made on heads of companies. They include the ability to act in the best interests of the whole enterprise and to strike the right balance in the conflicts of leadership. Too many organizations decentralize their operations without providing managers with knowledge which they need to perform their tasks or which would greatly improve their chances of success. This is one of the reasons why decentralization is seen to work well in easy times, but seldom in difficult times.

The whole idea of decentralization is to utilize the advantages of small scale. This calls for carefully considered action based on all relevant aspects, not just on the leader's desire to be king of the castle.

CENTRALIZATION V. DECENTRALIZATION IN RELATION TO THE COCE MODEL

The prime motive for decentralization is that of matching your offering as closely as possible to what *customers* want. Leaders of businesses and organizations must constantly struggle with the balance between productivity and customer-perceived value. This is much harder to do optimally if the leader is distanced from the customers. In a decentralized organization, the decisions are made in close alliance to customers, which improves the level of service. It is, however, necessary to have defined terms of reference.

From the *owners'* standpoint the issue of centralization v. decentralization involves a serious risk of upsetting the balance between productivity and customer-perceived value. If centralization is carried too far, the interests of productivity may predominate at the expense of value. Conversely, too much decentralization can lead to extravagant use of resources and over-delivery of service. The ownership aspect is considered here from the standpoint of profitability. Well-managed large corporations with concentrated ownership are often characterized by a high degree of decentralization within a strict framework of central rules.

Decentralization naturally implies delegated responsibility for both axes of the Efficiency Graph. Good times encourage demands for more delegated responsibility from managers who are sometimes short on ability to manage *costs* when tougher times arrive. Central production to take advantage of economies of scale must be balanced against delegated responsibility and motivation to improve productivity and reduce costs.

For *employees*, decentralization means greater responsibility for a larger part of the enterprise; this encourages motivation and energy, as well as enhances skills, and is thus the natural upside which is sometimes over-emphasized in the public sector. What is sometimes overlooked is the importance of responsibility for the whole, with a consequent risk of sub-optimization. It is often difficult to define delegated responsibility in such a way as to safeguard the best interests of the whole in all situations. The unfortunate result is that managers and employees act according to the way their performance is measured rather than for the good of the whole enterprise. Experience shows, however, that managers who act for the good of the whole are eventually promoted, even though they sometimes make decisions counter to the immediate interests of their own areas of responsibility.

Try this exercise:

Have you analysed the question of which functions ought to be run centrally and which locally?

Are there any unrealized economies of scale which could possibly be gained by a change of organization?

Are there any centrally run operations at present which would benefit from being decentralized? When considering this question, put yourself in top management's shoes, not those of the decentralized unit.

What has the general trend been in your organization over the past ten years? Towards centralization or towards decentralization?

8
Market Economy v. Planned Economy

People tend to regard the times in which they live as a period of transition. Such, indeed, is almost always the case, though perhaps even more so at the present time than ever before. The historian Peter Englund has pointed out that we human beings have a tendency to assign breaks in trends to calendar decades and centuries simply because evolution has equipped us with ten fingers. We rationalize developments and say that such-and-such was characteristic of the 1980s, the 1950s or the eighteenth century.

In actual fact, epochs begin and end without regard to the powers of ten on which we base our system of counting. The nineteenth century lasted up to the outbreak of World War I in 1914. By the same reasoning we can say that the twentieth century ended with the fall of the Berlin Wall and the collapse of the planned economies of the Eastern Bloc in 1989–90, for the issue that dominated our age was the struggle between planned and market economies.

That issue was finally resolved without a nuclear holocaust when the planned economies collapsed under the weight of their inability to provide what people need, namely economic prosperity, and personal and spiritual freedom. It marked the end of an epoch in which it was believed that the productivity axis of the Efficiency Graph was the only one worth considering. A planned economy is one designed to optimize productivity

without regard to customer utility. The paradox is that it failed
to do even what it was designed to do.

The subject of a planned economy has been raised in this book
because a large proportion of our economy, including most of
what goes on inside a company or organization, operates under
planned-economy conditions.

Leadership behaviour in a planned economy is dominated by
three major factors:

1   Division of labour to maximize productivity.
2   Lack of understanding of entrepreneurship.
3   Excess demand with associated mass production.

The economist Adam Smith advanced theories of the division of
labour in which people were regarded as substitutes for ma-
chines, while F. W. Taylor, an engineer and machining specialist,
refined the theory of maximizing productivity through strict
specialization of labour and reduction of the individual worker's
area of responsibility.

Since the days of the French physiocrats there has been an
awareness of a lack of key elements of knowledge explaining the
nature and origins of enterprise. It was long believed that enterprise occurred spontaneously if the following three conditions existed:

1   Workers to perform the labour.
2   Capital to finance the operation.
3   Bosses to supervise the work.

This notion prevailed far into the twentieth century, and had a
predominant influence on regional development policies, for example. Only after recent motivational research, pioneered by
David McLelland, was it realized that it also takes:

● risk-taking
● a high level of energy
● powerful performance orientation

for an enterprise to arise, grow and survive.

The total victory of the market economy over planned economy is an historical fact. The fall of the Berlin Wall and the collapse of the terror regimes of the Eastern Bloc in 1989–90 have brought us into a new epoch marked by a strong belief in the blessings of the market economy, except in a few planned-economy enclaves like Cuba and North Korea. Even China is slowly and convulsively transforming itself into a market economy.

The neo-liberal gospel dominates economic theory worldwide to such an extent that private capitalism is confused with market economy and socialism with planned economy. Though strong correlations naturally exist between these two pairs, they are by no means synonymous. It is quite possible to conceive of a socialist market economy (state capitalism) or a capitalist planned economy; something approaching the latter exists in corporative systems like those of France and Sweden.

My reason for raising the subject of market and planned economy here is to highlight the effects of the new epoch – not on the global economy and politics, but on thinking in companies and organizations. For most, organized activity is still subject to the rules of planned economy, in the sense that goods and services are delivered to users who do not have a free choice of suppliers.

This is true not only in the tax-financed public sector but also in commercial companies where internal deliveries of goods and services are made to users who have no other option. A line manager in an airline is not free to decide which pilots, cabin crews or aircraft he or she wants to use. Austrian Airlines, for example, cannot choose Russian pilots (who cost fifteen times less), flight attendants from Air France or aircraft from British Airways.

The same conditions prevail in most EU countries. Europe is full of organizational structures that operate under planned-economy conditions. This was one of the reasons why the European Union was formed.

On the few occasions when I have met leaders from liberated Eastern countries like Poland and Latvia, I have encountered an attitude of amazement at the phenomenon of the market economy. How, they wonder, can such an apparently chaotic system be superior to a well-ordered, rational planned economy? A planned economy has a number of characteristics that resemble the blessings of technocracy:

1 *Production can be ideally planned.* Supply is regulated by the production process instead of having to be adjusted to demand. This gives a high degree of rationality in production.
2 *Transaction costs are much lower.* If you can avoid market transactions and make internal transactions only, you can set up long-term agreements that eliminate the need for the protracted negotiations involved in market transactions.
3 *A vertical integration chain can be maintained.* Combines and similar ear-of-corn-to-loaf-of-bread systems minimize sales processes and transportation.
4 *Production is optimally rationalized.* Experience Curve effects are achieved. Products can be manufactured in long runs, with economies of scale in all functions.
5 *Research and development (R & D) are rationalized.* With no need for parallel development of many variants, there is no duplication of R & D costs.
6 *The sales function is free from the enormous over-capacity that exists in market economies.* Over-capacity in the retail sales force is estimated at between 400 and 500%. This apparent irrationality does not occur in planned economies.
7 *The route to efficiency in a planned economy lies in producing goods cheaply with a highly rationalized production apparatus.* Quality and customer utility do not control, nor are they regarded as essential. The main object is to fill a need for a basic function.

Highly educated people in companies and organizations tend to reason along these lines. Large corporations have a tendency to develop into mini-Soviet Unions and to grow technocratic and ever more self-satisfied. Companies pursue the goal of integration, i.e. an ever-increasing proportion of the value of what they sell is made in their own factories. Market transactions give way to internal transactions.

Herein lies the background to the Nobel Prize in economics that was awarded in 1991 to Ronald Coase for his article *The Nature of the Firm*. In this famous article he advanced a theory of the expansion of companies. The essence of the theory was that it is transaction costs which determine whether it pays to conduct a given activity within a company or to buy it from elsewhere. It is significant that Coase received his Nobel Prize for an article written in 1937, a time when the planned economy had just foundered.

One example is General Motors (GM) which has long had the highest degree of integration in the automotive industry. In-house added value accounts for 65% of the price of a GM car in the United States. This means that GM makes a large proportion of its components – blinkers, transmissions, windows, etc. – in its own factories. GM's Components Division has had serious profitability problems, largely explained by the fact that market-economy mechanisms have been eliminated in favour of planned economy mechanisms. Business Week *has made a comparison with what Honda pays for its components in the United States, and found great differences to the disadvantage of GM.*

FREE CHOICE: THE KEY TO MARKET ECONOMY SUPERIORITY

The superiority of the market economy is not a matter of who owns business enterprises: it makes little difference whether the owners are a co-operative, private shareholders, a municipality or the State. The real reason for the superior efficiency of the market economy is that customers have a free choice of suppliers. A supplier who is not chosen, or chosen too seldom, must either grow more efficient and give customers better value, or else ultimately be forced out of business. This mechanism is lacking in much of the organized world, i.e. in all parts of systems which deliver to users who do not have a real and free choice of alternative suppliers.

The metamorphosis of a mass-production, mass-consumption society into one in which a shortage of goods no longer prevails changes the parameters by which operations are controlled. Productivity, which is favoured in the first instance by the rationale of long production runs and a planned economy, becomes less relevant. By contrast, the importance of the value axis – quality as a function of price – increases dramatically. Control is much more complicated when the rationality of economies of scale must be weighed against the irrationality of customers' preferences.

The Efficiency Matrix is central to this discussion. It is shown again in Figure 8.1 to refresh the reader's memory. You can achieve efficiency by manipulating either of the two axes of the graph. With a given cost structure you can increase value to customers and thus boost demand both quantitatively and qualitatively, i.e. to get a better price. You can also improve efficiency by reducing your labour, overhead and/or capital costs. In actual practice it is rarely a matter of one axis or the other but of both, though the degree to which value or productivity can be influenced may be of decisive importance.

The actual aim of a planned economy is to maximize productivity with no special regard paid to quality. To take the former Soviet Union as an example at national level, one of the tasks of a mass-consumption society was to provide the population with footwear. Here the basic need to supply goods was the overriding consideration: a pair of shoes, regardless of what they are like, is better than no shoes at all.

In such a situation planned-economy thinking is irresistibly seductive. We build three gigantic footwear combines: one in Siberia, one in the Caucasus and one in a western republic such as the Ukraine or Belarus. These combines are vertically integrated, with everything

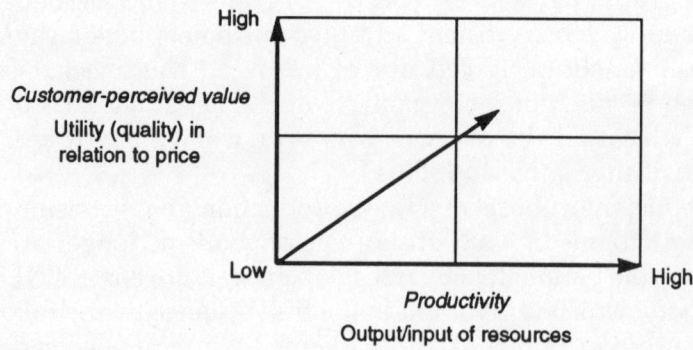

Figure 8.1   *Efficiency Matrix.*

from cattle-breeding and tanneries to mass production of finished shoes. Since the basic footwear function is the prime consideration, and since the aim is to attain high production capacity at low cost, we manufacture only two models – one black and one brown, but otherwise of identical design.

By backward integration within the combines we avoid all transaction costs between purchasing and sales organizations. Product development can be concentrated, and all the economies of scale lie within reach.

At the same time we integrate forward by setting up a Union-wide shoe sales chain. We open a thousand monopoly shoe shops as the sole source of footwear for all Soviet citizens – naturally too few to cover the whole empire. Since people's use of their time is not an item in the National Budget, it is better to let citizens queue for their shoes because then productivity can be maximized at the retail end too. The productivity of shoe salespeople is bound to be extremely high when they never have to stand around waiting for customers but can devote the whole of the day to productive work.

The paradox is that the planned economies of the East did not deliver goods of the quality that people wanted, neither did they produce enough to satisfy demand. The system was not capable of fulfilling the basic supply-of-goods function nor of producing goods cheaply.

A good example of the ineffectuality of a planned economy on both axes of the Efficiency Matrix is the production of the foul-smelling little East German Trabant, whose pre-World War II origins were the same as those of Audi. During the GDR era the Trabant works had a waiting-list of up to six years for those who wanted to buy its cars, but after the reunion of the German States, which enabled East Germans to choose other models, nobody wanted to buy a Trabant any more. Planned economy, in other words, is a system that is incapable of producing even what people do not want to buy anyway.

Under pressure of hardening competition and the realization of the inadequacies of planned economies, the world's leaders are now seeking ways to do something about efficiency in parts of organizations that operate under planned-economy conditions. This explains the rise of new methods and approaches like benchmarking, total quality management (TQM), make-or-buy analysis, business process re-engineering (BPR), zero-base planning, and so on.

The synthesis of experience from a planned economy and Ronald Coase's Nobel Prize makes the balance between a market and planned economy a central issue. This applies especially to all the competition-sheltered systems that exist in Europe. European civil aviation, as expressed by a representative of Lufthansa, is used here to illustrate European inefficiency:

1   The United States is one air traffic control zone with 20 Air Traffic Centres (ATCs) all using the same system.
2   Europe has 22 air traffic control zones, 52 ATCs and a plethora of systems.
3   Europe's 52 centres operate 31 different systems using hardware from 18 suppliers, 20 operative systems and 40 programming languages.
4   Delays increased by 21% during 1973 to 106,000 hours, equivalent to twelve years.
5   Lufthansa's aircraft logged 13,700 hours in holding patterns, burning 50,000 tonnes of fuel.
6   Passengers spent 14,600 aircraft-hours in planes on the ground awaiting clearance from ATCs.
7   Lufthansa paid 500 million marks in ATC fees, landing fees, etc. These fees are rising at an annual rate of about 20%, while service is steadily deteriorating.

One of the many reasons for the low productivity of European airlines is the need of governments to top up their depleted exchequers by charging exorbitant fees. Failure to utilize economies of scale, aggravated by fiscal policies, thus imposes undue hardship on many industries including civil aviation.

There are many arguments in favour of the freedom of choice that is the driving force of efficiency in market economies. Neoliberals, however, intone the liturgy of market economy to a point where they provoke a powerful counterreaction, primarily from the advocates of public monopolies. The reason is that the pendulum, as in many other cases, has swung so far in the other direction that the results are often questionable or downright bad. This is extremely unfortunate, as it gets in the way of a reasoned debate. Exaggeration gives public monopolies, which definitely need to be challenged, the ammunition they need to defend their continued enjoyment of undisturbed freedom from competition.

MOCK MARKET ECONOMY

Recognizing the superiority of market transactions in promoting efficiency, many companies try to simulate a market economy by setting up "autonomous" subsidiaries and internal pricing systems. However, these measures fail in many cases to satisfy the basic criterion that market economy is conditional upon the ability of the buyer or user of goods and services to choose freely between alternative suppliers. The following is an example:

A while ago my firm had a consultancy assignment for a large transport company with two operative divisions: passenger and goods traffic. Our principal was the goods traffic division, the smaller of the two.

These divisions were operated as separate profit centres with a large number of shared functions. One such function was data processing which had been working for the past three years to construct a new production control system. The project had already incurred heavy costs.

After three years the data processing department wanted to review the budget for the project with the goods division. Its budget for the current year was charged with the sum of 6 million pounds, a figure which infuriated the general manager of the division; he demanded an estimate from the data department of how much further investment would be needed to complete the project. The estimate came to a total of 17 million pounds over a period of three years.

Although the divisional management in theory had a free choice of system suppliers, no such freedom existed in fact. In view of the grotesque proportions of the situation, the division insisted on being allowed to purchase data processing services from an external source. The question was passed all the way up to the top management of the group which, with great reluctance and for the first time in the history of the group, finally consented to allow the division to invite competitive bids.

This is one of many examples of what we can call fake commercialization – a mock market economy without the prime requisite of a free choice of supplier. All internal pricing systems, companizations of departments, etc. are meaningless gestures if there is no freedom of choice.

In Chapter 4 we considered some of the approaches that can be adopted to promote efficiency in the absence of a market economy. The most readily adaptable approach is benchmarking, i.e. systematic comparison with and learning from example. The advantage of this method is that it can be applied to both axes of the Efficiency Graph, preferably in combination with TQM or BPR. This not infrequently results in a make-or-buy analysis to determine whether a given activity ought to be retained in-house or bought from an external source.

All functions and processes that a company ought to handle itself should also be subject to an efficiency appraisal. Consider what examples from outside could be adopted as models for a benchmarking exercise.

MARKET ECONOMY V. PLANNED ECONOMY IN RELATION TO THE COCE MODEL

Market economy means that *customers* or users have a free choice of suppliers. Planned economy is justified in many cases, particularly where market transaction costs would otherwise be too high. An employee cannot negotiate with his or her employer every morning over pay and conditions of employment for that day's work. Such conditions are best regulated by a long-term contract in which the employee is regarded as a supplier and the employer as a customer.

The question of *ownership*, as I have already pointed out, is distinct from that of the system under which an organization operates. Analytically speaking, the superiority of the market economy is not a function of ownership but of the customer's/user's freedom to choose between alternatives. The owner naturally has an overriding interest in efficient operations which favour market transactions. This, however, is often counterbalanced by the owners' ambition to own a larger company which encourages integration and numerous internal relationships of a planned-economy nature.

Two opposing forces likewise influence *costs*. High transaction costs argue in favour of planned-economy relationships with a view to reducing costs. The counter-force, again, is the user's free choice between alternative suppliers. This choice promotes efficiency, i.e. customer-perceived value in relation to productivity and thus to costs.

Employees are affected insofar as a large element of market transactions contributes to higher efficiency and thus to job security, although the number of jobs may diminish during a transitional period. A planned economy is apt to lull employees into a false sense of security by letting them ignore the demands of efficiency. This, like three of the Seven Deadly Sins – Lechery, Gluttony and Sloth – feels good initially. Employees have a long history of trying to resist the market's constant pressure for efficiency. To many employees, like those of Air France or Deutsch Bundespost Telekom, the transition from planned to market economy feels threatening and uncomfortable.

Try this exercise:

Are there any functions or activities in your enterprise that are not actually part of your core skills?

List five areas in your enterprise that are potential candidates for a shift from a planned to a market economy.

Make a list of areas in which a planned economy does and should prevail, but which lack criteria of efficiency, i.e. creation of value in relation to productivity or cost.

Are there any core skills which your enterprise currently buys from outside but which, from a strategic standpoint, ought to be supplied from within the organization?

9
Business Management v. Capital Management

The conflict of business management v. capital management applies primarily to companies, i.e. to organizations whose existence is based on the profit motive, whereas the other conflicts discussed in the book apply to all forms of organized activity.

The essence of the profit motive is that the difference between the realized value and the cost of realizing it must be as large as possible within a defined time frame. The question of the time frame, i.e. the balance between maximized present value and maximized value over a longer period of time, is another conflict that has already been dealt with in Chapter 3. I have elected to deal with the issue of business management v. capital management because the two are often confused, obscuring the division of roles among the parties concerned and – even worse – obscuring the aims of the organization.

DIFFERENCE IN KIND BETWEEN ENTERPRISE AND ADMINISTRATION

Enterprise is a word borrowed from the French. Like its Anglo-Saxon cognate *undertaking*, it implies an active, purposeful initiative in contrast to the administration of capital assets by, say, an investment company, a conglomerate or a pension fund. The anonymization of ownership and its separation from business are often crucial factors in the nature and development of a company. A capital-managing owner is a gambler on the financial market and seldom, if ever, feels any real commitment to the company's vision or business mission.

Players on the financial market like the objects of their administration to be dependable and prefer to invest their capital in stable, mature industries. Companies that come under institutional ownership tend to develop a management culture that is oriented towards serving the financial interests of their owners rather than supporting their customers and employees. Costs and productivity become tools for serving the financial interests of owners, as illustrated in the following example.

The American conglomerate ITT includes the Sheraton hotel chain, a large division that manufactures automotive components and defence materiel and a luxury casino called the Desert Kingdom in Las Vegas. In addition, ITT conducts financial operations through ITT Hartford Group Inc. The slaughter value of ITT was estimated in May 1994 at 115 dollars per share, which is 15 cents above the stock market quotation.

ITT has been headed since 1982 by Rand V. Araskog. During his first eight years at the helm the management was subjected to increasingly vociferous criticism from its institutional owners, who included the Californian pension fund Calpers, for the poor performance of its stock. The company had divested itself of its original core business by selling its Telecom Division to Alcatel.

Calpers' criticism eventually led the Board to change the system of remuneration for top management; executives' salaries were related to the quoted price of the company's stock.

This had·a remarkable effect on share prices which rose by 50% in the two years from 1991. Trading profits, however, remained low. Operating profits in the various business units did not rise at all. Instead, the management of the group devoted its energies to raising the share price by realizing assets and making a major effort in the fields of public and investor relations. Executives also made heavy stock purchases on their own account, which is legal in the United States. A sizeable proportion of the increase in profit per share, 23%, was thus accounted for by the company's purchase of 28 million shares from the market.

The greatest weakness of conglomerates is a lack of feeling for, and long-term commitment to, their component companies. In the case of ITT, the conglomerate structure is compounded by a diffuse institutional ownership which regards stock-market prices as the prime criterion of success.

THE UNSATISFACTORY COMPROMISE OF VENTURE CAPITAL

The clearly defined objective of an enterprise, usually formulated as a vision or corporate mission, is often compromised by demands for return on invested capital. Capital managers look for companies with a clear vision and a commitment to development. Their aim is to invest in seed companies in order to increase the return on their capital as the companies evolve from seed via business development to growth and maturity. The S curve in Figure 9.1 illustrates the process.

What capital managers want is to ride the wave of seed companies' growth. By doing so they dig dangerous pitfalls for the seed companies when the latter need capital to expand. The

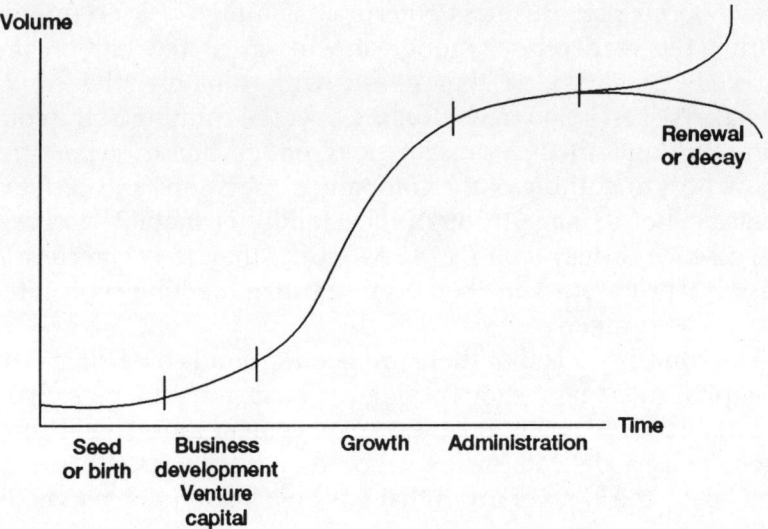

Figure 9.1 *The Process of a Company's Evolution From Seed to Maturity.*

long-term vision of the company's mission often has to give way to the new owners' short-term desire for a return on their capital. Here we have a built-in conflict which is hard to resolve. Constructive forms of venture capital financing are one of the most difficult things to secure in Western society today. The Swedish industrialist Curt Nicolin has put it thus: "Genuine venture capital is owned by individuals, not by institutions, co-operatives or the State. There are too many nervous people there who are afraid to go for broke."

This problem can be traced back to that of unemployment which, in turn, is a result of a number of major factors, including the industrial emergence of Southeast Asia, the liberation of Eastern Europe and over-ambitious welfare schemes. Different methods of venture capital financing are constantly being tried, but with extremely limited success. There are two main reasons for this:

1   Payback requirements are far too short-sighted.
2   Tax rules are formulated to favour companies but not their owners.

A company's explicit aim or corporate mission represents a heavy social risk. Business enterprise is a high-risk occupation during the seed phase, though it wins great recognition if it succeeds in surviving that phase. Unfortunately, the capital managers exercise a large influence over the running of the company through their representatives on its board, who often know next to nothing of the company's operations and can do a great deal of damage through their failure or inability to grasp the essence of its *raison d'être*. At worst, they may interfere in business processes and thereby jeopardize the long-term interests of the company.

The conclusion is that there are good grounds for being wary of capital managers' shortcomings as business managers. Striking a balance between business management and capital management is a delicate task for boards of directors. Reasoning leads us to the view of profit that has long been characterized by a focus on return on investment. Should we agree with Peter Drucker that "profit is the cost of staying in business", or should we take the opposite stance and regard profit primarily as a return on working capital?

Transactional economy seems to exert a spellbinding influence on businesspeople. Let us consider the case of a skilled carpenter who starts a building construction firm in the mid-1940s. The company buys and refurbishes some properties, and a few decades after its foundation it goes public. At the same time it separates into a construction division, a property management division and a financial division. Gradually the company has transformed itself from a successful building firm into a fat wallet. The Board starts to wonder what its core business actually is and decides to define itself as a property company. Property management leads to a progressive decline in the skills of building contracting which is now regarded as a sideline instead of the principal business.

The victims of the recent property market crash include many companies with a similar history.

THE OWNERS' REVOLT

There are signs abroad today of an incipient revolt by capitalists against the mediocracy of big-business management. At Calpers the legendary Dale M. Hanson, together with Richard H. Koppes, has striven to restore owners to corporate power. During the 1980s shareholders were regarded as being something of a necessary evil, and managements paid little or no attention to them. Dale Hanson assembled a few investors, primarily those in pension funds, at a number of meetings. Eventually these institutions succeeded in moving together against a mismanaged corporation – General Motors (GM). This resulted in a now-famous letter from Calpers to the GM management, which, in turn, resulted in the resignation of GM's Chief Executive Roger Smith. Dale Hanson commented that "He was able to talk and say nothing to us, which was quite a talent."

This unexpected action on the part of the capital managers accelerated planned measures to improve GM's profits. Perhaps this can be taken as a sign of a *rapprochement* between business and capital managers, if the latter are now demanding that large corporations raise their sights and exploit business opportunities better.

PAY OFF OR PLOUGH BACK?

Tetra Pak, IKEA and BMW are all examples of companies that have been managed with both empathy and success even when they have expanded. If the financial fruits of successful business management are viewed as a gift rather than as the result of hard work, there is a temptation to grow sloppy. Successful companies have learned to distinguish cash in hand from inward cash flow. Well-filled coffers tend to lower the level of ambition of large corporations, as in the case of ITT. The management slackens off and contents itself with reaping the dividends on capital, instead of using profits to develop the business in competition with others.

According to this view, a company like Volvo ought not to set return on investment (ROI) as its primary goal, but should generate profitability that will enable it to develop in a given direction. Rather than defining its goal as a given percentage above inflation averaged over a business cycle, it should express its goals in terms of development capability, such as:

1   We want to develop a van within the next two years and capture 8% of the American market in that segment.
2   As the world's most northerly automotive manufacturer, we want to reposition ourselves as the first choice for cold-climate motoring with four-wheel drive, aluminium bodies and related attributes.
3   We are going to invest in the Asiatic markets and make ourselves the first alternative to Japanese luxury cars.

Enterprise involves risk-taking and that, in turn, requires a cash flow to cover the risk and finance investment in business development.

We know that all strategic planning involves a built-in conflict between profitability and growth. This tends to be forgotten in periods when the economy is expanding fast. At such times demands are made for *both* high profitability *and* rapid growth, but the conflict cannot be wished out of existence.

In companies where the influence of capital managers is strong, growth is frequently neglected in favour of profitability. The reverse situation prevails where the majority ownership is truly committed to the company, i.e. today's profits are sacrificed to enable growth. This applies to companies like Tetra Pak, IKEA and BMW, as well as to several other well-known companies before they reached the point of needing an injection of capital to finance further growth.

Traditional key financial indicators often form the basis of performance standards in a world marked by institutional hunger for dividends. If excellent growth companies like IKEA, Tetra Pak, etc. had contented themselves with normal profits to satisfy institutionally inclined owners, their level of ambition would probably have been much lower and their rate of growth much slower.

All entrepreneurs have to face the dual challenge of building up solid financial strength without losing the entrepreneurial spirit and without being tempted to metamorphose into administrators. Yet the risk that success and capital strength may lead to repletion and loss of ambition must not be interpreted to mean that capital strength is a bad thing. On the contrary, the entrepreneur often views profit as a criterion of success rather than a reward as such.

This is something which the left-leaning political establishment fails to understand. The entrepreneur does not derive sustenance from profit-as-payment, but regards it instead as confirmation that value has been created which exceeds the cost of creating it. Punitive taxation of risk-taking entrepreneurs may bring in some money that can be distributed to others, but at the same time it obliterates the visible evidence of success. This undermines the motivation for further expansion, thereby inhibiting employment and growth.

A person who owns assets is also, generally speaking, a better businessperson. With sound finances to fall back on, the entrepreneur can afford to keep calm and wait out risky situations. Almost all successful entrepreneurs have shown an early instinct to strive for a high level of solvency.

In assessing return on capital we ought to ask ourselves what kind of capital we are looking for a return on. Is the traditional concept of working capital in fact relevant to actual business operations? As we all know, the skill component of all kinds of business enterprise has grown steadily larger, making traditional key indicators of return on capital steadily more obsolete. Should one, as a progressive business manager, try to assess the "invisible balance sheet"? And, in what time frame should success be judged? These questions gradually acquire philosophical connotations. Eventually the demand for dividends will come into conflict with the need for growth. Capital managers are primarily out for higher dividends and share price quotations, whereas entrepreneurs aim for growth and high market shares.

STRENGTH IN RESOURCES V. STRENGTH OF AMBITION

The dynamics of business exhibit a phenomenon that puzzles rational technocrats, namely the observed fact that ample resources in the form of a strong balance sheet, a high market share and a large volume of sales give no protection when an ambitious challenger enters the arena. A now-famous article entitled "Stretch and Leverage" by Gary Hamel and C. K. Prahalad in the March–April 1993 issue of *Harvard Business Review* dealt with this subject. The authors contrasted a number of powerful, resource-rich companies with others whose primary attributes were high levels of ambition and motivation. Their conclusions were astonishing, but perhaps not so surprising in hindsight.

Hamel and Prahalad illustrated their argument by contrasting two companies competing in the same industry. Typical examples were Pan American Airlines v. American Airlines in the 1980s and Philips v. Sony in the 1960s. The dominant company (PanAm/Philips) was the leader in its field and had accumulated vast resources of all kinds: skilled employees, high technology, well-known brands, a widespread network of distributors, a high market share and a stable cash flow. The company had reached the top of its tree, and its ambition was to defend its market share and earn an average of 10–15% on its capital over a business cycle.

The challenger (American Airlines/Sony) was a relative latecomer to the industry and was much smaller than the leader. It had to make do with fewer employees, less capital, a lower R & D budget and a much smaller distribution network. The challenger, however, was much more ambitious; its ultimate aim was to take over the leadership of the industry.

Few objective observers would bet on the challenger in this situation. This is a view that has characterized strategic thinking for many years. Access to resources, rather than level of ambition, has been regarded as the crucial success factor. This is why acquisitions, mergers, etc. have been viewed as effective instruments for creating stable and viable business structures. The amalgamation of Sweden's steelworks and proposals to merge Volvo and Saab are typical examples.

What Hamel and Prahalad call "misfit" is the gap between the challenger's resources and ambitions. This stress factor in competition acts in itself as a driving force powerful enough to move mountains.

If we look at the affluence of the established market leader and the ambitions of the challenger, we can easily imagine what their competitive strategies will look like. The leader must rely on traditional "strategic" behaviour and head off the challenger by utilizing its capital strength. The principal options are price cuts and investment in higher market share and R & D. The leader ought to be able to sit back and view the situation calmly, confident of being able to out-compete the challenger whenever he or she chooses. This is exactly the situation in which many European airlines find themselves today. Scandinavian Airlines System, for example, has declared itself capable of wiping out its competitor Transwede at any time. This view resembles that which prevailed during World War I: "The side that runs out of ammunition first will lose."

The challenger adopts guerrilla tactics, seeking out niches rather than mounting frontal attacks on its competitor's well-defended main markets. This is not the classic case of the smaller and more nimble company beating the bigger and slower-moving one; it is the gap between the challenger's resources and ambitions that boosts its motivation to an extremely high level. The leader, on the other hand, does not have enough of a gap between ambition and resources. So what beat companies like PanAm and Philips was not lack of resources, but lack of ambition.

High ambition and willingness to take risks are the very definition of entrepreneurship which can thus be said to be one of the bottleneck resources of business management – especially in the case of large, well-established companies whose primary goal is normal return on capital over a business cycle.

FORCE OF CIRCUMSTANCE V. FORCE OF WILL

The issue of resources v. ambition is closely akin to that of external circumstances v. individual will or, to use the technical terms, of determinism v. voluntarism.

Determinism, derived from the Latin *determinare* which means to set limits, is a school of philosophy which proceeds from the power of circumstances over individuals and situations. According to deterministic thought, human decisions and actions are always constrained by prevailing circumstances and free will does not exist. Voluntarism, from the Latin *voluntas*, which means will is a doctrine which holds that will is the innermost essence of being and that will completely shapes our reality.

Determinism has come to be the analytical foundation of traditional education in business administration throughout the world. The analysis, unfortunately, is often co-opted into the sole service of the administrators, and the deterministic view is incompatible with entrepreneurial behaviour.

This contrasts with will-driven entrepreneurship represented by the challengers of this world. These are companies which ignore facts that ought to deter them from the ventures they undertake. I myself once started a company to manufacture pre-fabricated foundation elements; fortunately I neglected to make the analyses that would have emphatically advised me against starting the company.

ENTERPRISE AND ADMINISTRATION IN RELATION TO THE COCE MODEL

To *customers*, administration means high prices with the compensation of a safe buy. You cannot go wrong if you buy IBM. The challenger, on the other hand, is more dynamic and therefore frequently delivers better value. The classic motto of the Avis car rental company, "We try harder" defines the contrast precisely. It stands for the aim of the smaller but more ambitious company to give better customer satisfaction than its dominant competitor (Hertz).

Administration offers *owners* security. Lack of ambition means that no risks are taken. This makes ownership safe, albeit rather unexciting. By contrast, we have entrepreneurial risk-taking that combines a high level of ambition with a high level of risk. Administrators deeply dislike risk-taking, except marginally to add spice to an otherwise safe portfolio.

Costs are generally treated with much greater respect by entrepreneurs than by administrators. Ability to manage resources is in fact the key competitive advantage which the entrepreneurial company holds compared to the administered company. The former generally gets much more value out of every pound, mark or dollar it spends than does the latter. The classic example is Philips which failed to get value from the investments that it had made. IBM is another example of inefficient resource management that led to low productivity.

An administrative corporate culture tends to encourage power orientation in its *employees*. It attracts people who put their own interests ahead of those of the business. Conversely, entrepreneurial organizations attract performance-oriented people who derive their satisfaction from contributing to the success of the business. Working in a business-oriented entrepreneurial culture is naturally more conducive to motivation than working in a static administrative culture.

Try this exercise:

Has there been any tendency over the past ten years in your enterprise to over-emphasize the administrative side of management at the expense of entrepreneurship or its equivalent?

Do you tend to set goals in financial rather than operative terms? (The latter are defined as goals which translate the corporate mission into practice and contribute to realizing a vision.)

Does your organization see itself as the big, fat, well-fed cat that relies on its vast resources, or as an aggressive and ambitious challenger?

Would you assign your competitors to the large-resource or high-ambition categories?

10
Thought v. Action

In the balance between thought and action we can discern a pattern in time. There have been periods when thought has taken second place to action, and vice versa. In a world that is to all appearances fairly stable, thought often gains the upper hand at the expense of action. During the period after World War II, world business and consumption patterns were dominated by demand surplus and production shortage. These patterns seemed so remarkably stable that strategic planning came to be interpreted as making choices between options for growth.

This period of relative stability nurtured a pattern of leadership focused on analysis and planning. Too much faith was placed in planning techniques, while dynamics were ignored. Posterity has characterized that epoch by phrases like "paralysis through analysis". Companies and public-sector bodies set up planning departments whose duty was to make forecasts of future developments and to put forward options for future action based on these, using mathematical techniques to optimize the results.

Operations analysis, in particular, came to play a prominent part as an aid to optimizing choices between alternative courses of action. Operations analysis is a collective name for a number of mathematical techniques which are used to check and optimize decision situations involving a large number of parameters. These techniques include linear programming, decision trees, Monte Carlo simulations, queuing theory, critical paths, and so on. The purpose was to achieve the best possible solution in a given set of circumstances. Operations analysis, however, cannot influence the circumstances, and is therefore best suited for use in stable situations.

This epoch of leadership came to a catastrophic end when the oil shocks of the 1970s rudely destroyed most of the planning techniques that had been developed. The predictability of trends was demolished at one stroke, putting a premium on fast foot-work and readiness to act.

The 1980s saw a massive denunciation of earlier theories of leadership. Professor Henry Mintzberg of McGill University at-tacked the intellectual Harvard School, while in Sweden Hans Werthén, CEO of Electrolux, coined a phrase about the need to parry rather than plan. Intellectual exercise was pilloried in this decade which came to be partly symbolized by the book *In Search of Excellence* published in 1981 by Tom Peters and Robert Waterman. It emphasized commitment to customers and get-up-and-go as the criteria of leadership. Slogans like "Try it, fix it, do it" were fashionable, and were quickly adopted by organiza-tions with a broad spectrum of cultural backgrounds.

The 1980s were dominated in many countries by the myth of action as a recipe for success. Decisive action and fearless for-ward drive became the overriding principles in most organiza-tional cultures, though they were often disguised under more academic terminology. Many companies seized upon a strategic idea that was actually the result of action already taken, not of something that had preceded action.

THE RIGHT IDEAS IN THE RIGHT ORDER

The matter of order is of crucial importance in the alternation of thought and action. Blind faith in action has often led to action preceding thought which almost invariably leads to disaster. There are some cases where thought has preceded action – albeit incorrect, while in others, both analysis and deep thinking were neglected. Both situations are quite common. Consider, for ex-ample, some of the things that Air France has done, for reasons known only to itself and God:

Despite precarious solvency, the management pushed through the acquisitions of Sabena, part of Continental Airlines, the Czech airline CSA and Air Inter. The flock mentality of the airline industry must have influenced the management to such a degree that the acquisitions were made without a thought to analysis of economies of scale, or to the willingness and ability of the French State to finance deficits. To an outside observer, the whole thing looks like a manifestation of gung-ho empire-building mentality without benefit or forethought.

Another example from aviation illustrates vision and power of thought marred by insufficient prior analysis. A thought, in other words, may be profound and well formulated, but still be wrong.

Such was the case with Scandinavian Airlines System (SAS) which decided to integrate ground transportation, air travel and hotel accommodation in a package offering to business travellers. The SAS' management's feeling for the situation was born of experience from the package tours business. In its eagerness to create a competitive advantage, SAS bundled a number of components without prior analysis of the intended target group's buying behaviour. The result was yet another in the long line of bastard ideas sprung from the expansive ambitions of managements' rather than from customers' perceptions of goods and services. This idea, too, was clothed in strategic verbiage, but it was an idea that proceeded outward from inside the company instead of vice versa.

Again and again we can witness how companies try to sell more by bundling goods and services. The error is that the prime motivational force is the company's desire to expand, and not the needs and wishes of its customers. Without the urge to expand there would be no development in the world, but the chances of success are greater if the urge is canalized with precision on the basis of customers' willingness to buy and pay. This illustrates the importance not only of thinking before acting, but also of getting the thoughts right. In this instance a fact base is a better guide than intuition or feeling. (See Chapter 5 for a discussion on this subject.)

Both companies and other organizations need to strike a balance between sticking to what they do best and broadening their scope of delivery in terms of offering (goods and services) or market served. In times when the trends are pointing upward there is a temptation to expand the scope of delivery unduly. This phase is eventually followed by a cry of "Back to basics!" or other such quotations of proverbs.

KEEPING THE CORPORATE MISSION IN SIGHT

Business management and leadership of organizations involve a constant debate on the respective merits of keeping with core business to taking risks and expanding – the latter being essential to development. The corporate mission is the framework within which energy should be channelled to maximize the probability of success. That energy is channelled most effectively if action is guided by the corporate mission.

It is, therefore, extremely important for organizations to define a corporate mission and stay with it until they make a deliberate, considered decision to change it. A corporate mission is composed of the following elements:

- Needs
- Customers
- Offering of goods and/or services
- Competitive advantage

Repeated use of the corporate mission as a touchstone curbs flamboyance in times of prosperity. It restrains the temptation to widen the scope of delivery, and is a support when the company needs to reduce its degree of integration and sell off or shut down parts of its operations.

The corporate mission has another, more offensive function. It encourages management to think through the elements of definition and exploit all the opportunities that a corporate mission offers. Broadening the geographical market served, for example, is often a highly successful route. It enables a corporate mission to be exploited on a larger market without risking departure from the core skills on which the company's success has been built.

THOUGHT AND FEELING

Feeling has played an exceptionally large part in the development of organizations. There are a number of examples from the 1980s. Edzard Reuter ran Daimler-Benz according to an unswerving philosophy of conglomeration, integrating aviation and information technology with the automotive core business. After some disastrous years of falling profits and shrinking market shares, the group is now struggling to free itself from the stranglehold of diversification.

There are other examples of strategic flock behaviour: General Motors acquired the EDS data consultancy company and the Hughes aviation company. British Aerospace bought the Rover Group, while Saab in Sweden builds aircraft and has also been involved in computer technology development. Strategic flock behaviour can be observed in every industry, and one may wonder why this is so.

Feeling often corrupts reason in a way that sometimes leads to major disasters. Failure to base action on rigorous thought has driven people to marvels of megalomania, i.e. to disastrously inefficient projects which nevertheless culminated in enduring monuments to achievement. The Great Wall of China, the Panama Canal and the Sydney Opera House are examples:

The world's largest structure, the only work of man that can be seen from the moon, is the 6,000-kilometre-long Great Wall of China. Though rebuilt and extended over the years, it was originally erected as a fortification to keep the nomad tribes out of the Middle Kingdom. Though it cost uncounted human lives and huge sums of money and resources, it was a failure as a line of defence. The principal function that it actually performed was to hold the vast Chinese empire together.

The Panama Canal was built by Ferdinand de Lesseps, a French diplomat who had previously been project manager for the Suez Canal which had been completed in 1869. De Lesseps then embarked upon the construction of the Panama Canal which, barring only the Wall of China, was the world's most expensive infrastructure project. Construction time was estimated at twelve years, but it actually took thirty-four years to build. During its construction 25,000 workers died of malaria or the bites of venomous snakes, spiders and scorpions. Upon completion in 1914, the total cost of construction was worked out at approximately fifty-five times the original estimate. The French canal company went bankrupt, ruining many small French investors who had put their savings into it and sparking off one of France's long succession of political scandals. The United States subsequently took over the project, establishing the new State of Panama as a US protectorate by peremptorily annexing a piece of Colombia.

The Sydney Opera House has come to stand as a symbol for the kind of creative cost estimation which seems to be at best the result of a runaway imagination and at worst a deliberate deception undertaken to get the project started. Self-deception, wishful thinking or analytical incompetence? It is difficult to tell.

Sydney is Australia's largest city and its Opera House, designed by Danish architect Jørn Utzon, was costed at 7 million Australian dollars with a projected construction period of five years.

The building was completed in 1973, sixteen years after work had started, and ultimately cost over 100 million Australian dollars, fifteen times more than estimated. That record is hard to beat, even when compared to the Concorde, the Seikan Tunnel in Japan (the world's longest), or more modest megaflops like the Eurofighter.

If it were not for the Wall of China, one might be tempted to suppose that action without foregoing thought is an Occidental trait. The fact that it is not confined to the West is confirmed by the following case of Japan Airlines:

Some members of Japan Airlines' cabin crews have salaries in the region of 80,000 dollars a year. The airline management had planned to make pay cuts but was stopped by the Japanese Ministry of Transport and Labour which openly threatened reprisals if the plans were put into effect.

At the same time it is illegal in Japan to use simulators for pilot training. At present pilots have to take their refresher courses in real aircraft, which cost 25,000 dollars per hour to operate compared to 1,000 dollars for the same time in a simulator.

The Japanese civil aviation authorities charge a fee of 10,000 dollars to land a Boeing 747 at Tokyo's Narita Airport – twice as much as in Frankfurt and more than four times as much as in New York.

In addition, Japan Airlines (JAL) is lumbered with an eleven-year contract with Boeing signed in 1985. Under this contract JAL has undertaken to buy aircraft from Boeing at a fixed exchange rate of 184 yen to the dollar. That is almost twice the current rate, and will have cost JAL two billion dollars extra by the time the contract expires in 1996.

The role of thought in relation to feeling and action is a difficult dilemma. One of the primary functions of the expert management consultant is to offer a "second opinion" in situations where feelings and the urge to act obscure reasoned thought. In enterprises exposed to normal criteria of efficiency, self-examination is a necessary condition for survival to a much greater extent than in enterprises of a more grandiose nature that spend other people's money. Publicly owned and operated enterprises obey somewhat different laws than those which apply to enterprises in which individuals are held responsible for efficiency.

Let us call this the Law of Irresponsibility. It applies to all who take risks for their own personal gain at the expense of their principals because they know they will never be held responsible if anything goes wrong, but they are able to take all the credit if their plans are successful.

This applies, for example, in municipal housing corporations, investment in refineries by state-owned oil companies, and new military aircraft projects. If the project goes on long enough, the people who supply the input for decisions can choose freely between taking the credit or moving elsewhere, thus avoiding personal responsibility. The same thing is obviously true in the political sphere. Countries like Sweden, Belgium and Italy are governed by political systems which, in the absence of personal responsibility, manipulate state finances in a manner inconsistent with the interests of the citizens, even though politicians are elected specifically to safeguard these interests.

It would be an act of human benefaction to strive for a system that links personal responsibility to authority delegated through universal suffrage or some other method. If only the problem were recognized, such forms of responsibilty would not be too difficult to devise.

Successful people tend to be corrupted by their success and the open admiration of those around them. The hazard of success lies in the old saying about pride going before a fall. Successful leaders are easily lulled into a false sense of security that tempts them to neglect thought and analysis.

When fact bases are ignored, it may be due to a combination of hubris and receptivity to ideas that are currently fashionable in the industry. This can make feeling a treacherous companion. What we call feeling consists of a combination of experience, over-confidence and trends. The danger is that feeling may grow into a substitute for thought rather than the complement that refines decision-making.

THE ROLE OF STRATEGY

The term "strategic planning" has come to symbolize an area of intellectual effort. In the stable, predictable world of the past the development of a company or organization was viewed as an exponential extrapolation of history. This reduced intellectual effort to a matter of plotting trends. In line with F. W. Taylor's ideas about division of labour, the task of long-term thinking was assigned to strategic planning staffs whose intellectual output was to be further processed in the line of operations. Thought and action were divorced.

Before the first oil crisis in 1974 there was a strong tendency to mechanize the task of strategy, i.e. the choice of long-term course. Action to satisfy short-term demands from planning technocrats became more important than strategic thinking. Strategy was centralized to planning staffs where no real strategic work ever took place. Their labours could at best be called strategic programming, i.e. conversion of strategic thinking into plans for action to be executed by others. The tasks of strategy were thus degraded and mechanized, to the great detriment of many companies.

This formalization of strategy led to a mechanized intelligence process which attempted to manage the unmanageable volumes of information that were produced. The stable course of events encouraged the belief that human intelligence could be replaced by artificial intelligence, expert systems, etc. Such formalized systems could indeed process more information in the form of hard data, but they lacked the ability to absorb and understand knowledge in depth, or to synthesize the mass of information. No actual learning ever took place, as was repeatedly pointed out by Henry Mintzberg and other critics of formalized strategic planning.

The formalized intellectual strategy process follows a sequence from analysis via data processing and administrative routines to, ultimately, implementation, strategy is also a process of learning. This process may be two-way or even reversed, for we think to act, but we also act to obtain input of experience to think about. Formal planning systems will never be able to predict discontinuities or come up with brilliant strategies. Instead of creating strategy, planning assumes that strategy already exists. According to Mintzberg, the concept of strategic planning is a fallacy. In actual fact, all that formal planning systems do is divide up implementation into phases after the strategy has been worked out.

To conclude, it is wrong to separate thought from action as the interplay between the two is very important. Individuals who possess first-hand information must think and translate their thoughts into action. That action must, in turn, lead to new insights which may need to be confirmed by analyses and subsequently may prompt new action, and so on. Patterns borrowed from the military do not work well in civilian life. A company cannot let a general staff plan a campaign to be fought by troops in the field. Business calls for give-and-take which promotes efficiency.

FROM VISION TO INSTRUCTION

In modern organizations there is a constant interplay of thought and action at all levels. Vision – "a memory of the future", as neurophysiologist David Ingvar calls it – represents the general concept which guides individual action in conjunction with thought. The visionary purpose is to inspire people with motivation and energy, in order to achieve more efficient development and increased job satisfaction.

Strategy, according to the more modern view, is action taken at the present time to assure future success. It is an expression of the will to achieve, differing from the corporate mission which is more an expression of the character and nature of the enterprise. Strategy is a specification of vision, whose purpose is to translate this very remote, and slightly diffuse, concept of vision into a pattern of present actions to be taken by an organization.

The structure of an organization can be divided into either functions or business processes. At present the business process view is gaining ground at the expense of functional thinking because processes are based on the customer need aspect, whereas functions are simply a breakdown of the organization into smaller units for purposes of manageability and specialization. When speaking of a process, what is intended is a business process as opposed to a function of an organization.

The breakdown into functions is an expression of the concept of the division of labour which dominated organizational theory during the age of mass production. Breakdown into functional areas should now be replaced by a process approach which involves identifying flows of products or services that create value for customers.

The formulation of long-term patterns of action for business processes or functions often requires more effort than that necessary for the whole. It requires the ability to see both the whole and its parts and to juggle both abstract thought and concrete phenomena. There is extremely little research or literature available on the long-term development of business processes. The following is an example from the telecommunications industry which is now being opened up to competition throughout Europe:

Invoicing, an apparently trivial process, has a strong influence on customers' choice of supplier. Despite operators' realization of this growing importance of the invoicing process, many operators seem incapable of co-ordinating this process properly and still divide invoicing routines among traditional functions, such as the accounting, data processing, marketing and legal departments. New competitors in the field naturally take advantage of this by devising more customer-friendly invoicing processes.

The transition from vision to instruction includes a monitoring phase which keeps a constant check on routine processes to ensure that they function properly. The timing of the transition from monitoring to action is difficult to judge; many leaders admit, after the fact, that they intervened too late. The following is a classic example from Aviation:

A Boeing 747 belonging to China Airlines had engine trouble at high altitude above the Pacific. The pilot, who in a modern aircraft monitors the flight, continued to monitor for so long that the aircraft went into a nosedive. The pilot just managed to pull out of it a bare thousand metres above the surface of the sea, and the plane finally made an emergency landing, having sustained severe damage to the fuselage. The subsequent commission of inquiry found that the pilot had continued to monitor the flight far too long instead of assuming control and taking corrective action.

Our human ability to construct theoretical systems sometimes leads us to adopt a passive attitude fostered by the apparent perfection of the system. The same thing happens in leadership. A finished set of instructions in the form of standards and procedural rules is a temptation to neglect or to fail to take action in situations where action is necessary. A typical, and topical, example is the passivity of a number of European governments with regard to their budgets. Loud warning voices about runaway budget deficits have long been heard in several countries.

Management by vision or management by instruction? That is the question. A thought embodied in a system becomes an instruction. Thought as a guide to action is called a vision or strategy. The world is governed not by one or the other, but by both.

THOUGHT V. ACTION IN RELATION TO THE COCE MODEL

Customers generally stand to benefit most from an action-oriented leadership. Willingness and ability to act are almost always directly linked to entrepreneurship and the focus on customers which it generates. The career pattern that exists in business and other organizations tends to reward intellectual ability rather than action. One of the weaknesses of large corporations is that the number of people in them who have direct dealings with customers is relatively fewer than in small organizations. Thought is often rewarded at the expense of action and this leads to customers being regarded as objects, i.e. as a necessary component in the conduct of business rather than the reason for being in business in the first place.

Owners are frequently represented by people whose interests are inclined towards the intellectual. It is for this reason that managements of badly-run enterprises are often left in place long after they should have been replaced. Owners are also influenced by the time factor. Active management often produces better profits in the short term, but this is not infrequently offset by sub-optimum management of the organization's long-term interests. Owners always claim to take the long view; the rules of the game require them to do so, however short-sighted their actual actions may be.

Active people are by far the best performers in the area of *costs*, although this is subject to reservations. There is a psychological advantage in a situation where costs are lower than revenues or the equivalent. In both national and corporate finance, the people who justify high present costs on the grounds that they contribute to future success are nearly always trying to fool both themselves and the organization. This almost always leads to dissatisfaction, loss of confidence in the leadership and suspicion that problems are being rolled on to the next generation of leadership. On the national level it gives rise to waves of speculation and interest-rate crises. In commercial companies, the pressure to act is much greater, although with the reservation that costs which are essential to future success must be carefully identified.

Employees tend to be the neutral party in this conflict. Employees behave in much the same way as leaders in the matter of thought v. action. All employees benefit from action that is preceded by thought and from sensitivity to signals. Action without thought and thought without action carry their own penalties in almost all situations.

Try this exercise:

Identify three situations in your enterprise where over-detailed analysis and difficulty in proceeding from analysis to action have damaged business.

Now try to identify three additional situations where over-eagerness to do something has led to sub-optimum action.

Identify two situations during the past ten years where decisions were prompted by feeling and conviction rather than rational analysis.

Consider what kind of changes in manning and organization might improve the behaviour of the enterprise in terms of thought and action.

11
Good Times v. Bad Times

War analogies frequently occur in the field of leadership. These analogies are seldom useful in practice, but they are appealing. Terms like frontal assault, guerrilla attack, market intelligence (i.e. espionage) and flank attack exert a strange fascination in situations where the analogy is incomprehensible or inappropriate.

The metaphors of war are applicable in one respect, namely in the concepts of peacetime generals and wartime generals. It is a long-established fact of military history that officers who are promoted in peacetime, according to the criteria then prevailing, are seldom the best leaders in wartime when other considerations apply. This is also true with civilian leadership.

This thesis is supported by innumerable military command situations past and present. The most illustrative example is that of the American General, Patton, in World War II. The film *Patton* with George C. Scott in the title role is recommended to interested readers. Quite apart from the instructive illustration, it is an exceptionally well-made film. The example is as follows:

Patton led the invasion of Sicily together with Field-Marshal Montgomery. In addition to his military qualifications, Patton was a history lecturer. During a visit to a military hospital he was so infuriated by the behaviour of a shell-shocked soldier that he struck him.

The scandal caused the Allied High Command to sack Patton on the spot. The Germans, however, believed that this was some sort of stratagem and never took Patton's dismissal seriously.

At the time of the invasion of Normandy Patton was reinstated by Dwight D. Eisenhower, and subsequently played a decisive part in two respects. First, he pushed his armoured forces right through the south of France and penetrated far behind the German lines. Second, he moved his whole tank army from southern France up to the Ardennes in November 1944 when the Germans launched their last desperate counter-attack. With a large American force surrounded and extremely poor weather, Patton drove his army from the south of France relentlessly for sixty hours to relieve the trapped American forces.

Patton was virtually impossible in peacetime; he displayed all the traits of an extremely entrepreneurial, performance-oriented person with an uncontrollable temperament, driving his men so hard that he was not a popular officer despite his successes.

At the close of the war Patton's army was the first allied force to reach Berlin. He sent a telegram announcing that the Soviet Union would be the next enemy and that he, therefore, proposed to drive on eastward. His superiors literally had to fly to Berlin and restrain him physically. He died shortly thereafter.

VISIONARIES AND OPERATORS

It is hard to find good compromises between well-integrated peacetime generals and aggressive, combative wartime generals. It is equally hard to find good compromises between inspiring visionaries capable of leading organizations and companies in good times, and tough, hard-nosed operators who can tackle urgent problems and make hard decisions in bad times.

The terms visionary and operator are used somewhat loosely here to describe different kinds of talent. The *visionary* is a person with a commitment to long-term development who has a conception of how the enterprise can reach certain unspecified far-off goals. The term is used here to describe persons whose main interest is in long-term business development.

The *operator*, by contrast, is a highly skilled tactician with the operative ability to achieve such things as high productivity at low cost, an efficient sales force, minimum capital tie-up and short throughput times.

These are not value-judgements. Both types of skill are necessary to run a company successfully over a period of time. The point is that the two types of skill are seldom, if ever, combined in equal proportions in one person. Just as the peacetime general performs poorly in combat, so the visionary lacks the ability to act decisively in times of crisis.

This line of reasoning leads to the inescapable conclusion that every period of an organization's development needs its own leader. That is not, however, what happens in practice. A leader who does a brilliant job in good times seldom relinquishes his or her post to somebody else when it is in the interest of the business to do so, nor does the combative operator willingly step aside to make way for the visionary business developer at what an objective observer would consider the appropriate time. Jan Carlzon did a splendid job of leading Scandinavian Airlines System (SAS) in its business development period from 1982, but the situation after the Kuwait crisis and in the recession that followed called for other capabilities in the head of an airline. It is of course easy to be wise after the event, but the visionary Carlzon ought to have left SAS long before circumstances forced him to resign.

There are, of course, exceptions to the rule. Håkan Frisinger, who led Volvo from a highly precarious situation to good profitability between 1976 and 1982, resigned as soon as the company started to generate a profit again. Just how voluntary his resignation was can be questioned, but the fact remains that Frisinger relinquished his position in the hope that it would be filled by somebody who could preside over a new period of business development.

A conflict exists between individuals who are equipped for visionary leadership in good times and those who are equipped for operative leadership in bad times. One can observe signs of an unfortunate counter-cyclic pattern in the appointment of executives in different situations. Just as armies promote good, decent, relations-oriented officers to general rank in peacetime, companies in good times appoint the type of executive who is unlikely to perform well in bad times.

Generals who achieve outstanding success because they are decisive, performance-oriented and aggressive in time of war

	Visionary	Technocrat/operator
Upturn	Does not cope well with coming downturn	Not good at business development, but useful in tough times
Downturn	Not a good operator, but needed when better times return	Good in a tight corner, but not good at exploiting the upturn

Figure 11.1   *Executive Types in Good Times and Bad Times.*

seldom if ever make suitable commanders in peacetime, when their action-oriented behaviour tends to be embarrassing. Similarly, bosses appointed in tough times are seldom ideally equipped to lead the company when it is doing well. The matrix in Figure 11.1 illustrates four typical situations.

In the square in the top left-hand corner of Figure 11.1 we find the visionary who is appointed at a time when things are going well and who succeeds in inspiring the organization and the people in it to take advantage of opportunities for development. The head of a business unit, for example, concentrates on product development, and on opening up new market segments and geographical markets. He or she is inclined to broaden the scope of delivery, i.e. to offer more goods and services to existing customers.

A visionary who is put in charge of a portfolio in good times, i.e. of managing a group of business units rather than being responsible for a single unit, will tend to go in for structural development. At best, the acquisitions and mergers will be concentrated to existing areas of business, i.e. synergistic. At worst, a visionary portfolio manager will go in for diversification. This is usually accompanied by claims of synergies in which neither employees nor the press place much faith.

When harder times come, as they always do, the company finds itself handicapped by a management that is poorly equipped to meet the new situation. The bottom left-hand square in Figure 11.1 represents this stage. Managing the transition from good times to bad times involves a very painful process of reorientation. An organization conditioned to prosperity always reacts to adversity too late. Its *laissez-faire* culture encourages slackness, complacency and lack of a sense of urgency. This represents a situation of adversity which calls for tough negative decision-making by a boss who was recruited in, and is best suited to, a period of prosperity and business development.

In hard times (the bottom right square in Figure 11.1), executives are appointed for their operative skills, i.e. their ability in terms of short-term efficiency. This is frequently achieved at the expense of long-term efficiency, but, in an emergency, problems need to be tackled in the right order. A company in a crisis situation lacks the resources to pursue long-term development policies which always generate more costs than revenues in the short and medium term. This type of executive is invaluable in difficult times because he or she possesses the moral courage and nowadays usually also the communicative ability that are needed to make tough decisions and to explain to people why those decisions must be made to safeguard the survival of the enterprise. At the present time in Western Europe, people are conditioned and prepared to accept explanations of that kind. The more people are aware of what is vital to the existence of the enterprise, the greater their readiness to listen to and accept decisions which in the short term cause hardship to themselves or their colleagues.

Leaders with these talents often, though by no means always, lack what it takes to run the organization in the subsequent period of prosperity (the top right square in Figure 11.1). The short view that was an asset in the crisis becomes a liability when things take a turn for the better. Calls for short-term profitability and exaggerated thrift can stifle new ventures and put an unwanted brake on the further development of the enterprise.

The top right-hand square in Figure 11.1 thus symbolizes the situation in which skilled operators are called upon to manage development processes of a more long-term nature. It is often difficult because people vary in their ability to optimize the time axis. This phenomenon is called time span capacity and has no relation to intelligence. The analogy with the current state of national finances in some major European countries is illustrative. Belgium, Sweden and Italy can be cited as examples of good-time cultures faced with different criteria for optimization as revenues fall and expenditures rise. Expansive, pork-barrel political leadership needs to be replaced by the prime virtues of austerity and thrift. Politics, just like business, needs a new kind of leadership embodied in a new set of leaders.

The same phenomenon is found in trade union movements all over Europe. Traditional, taken-for-granted union membership is gradually losing relevance as a result of the new industrial logic of the Western world. The spread of unemployment, the growing importance of information technology and the growing realization of why companies must be profitable are factors which have heavily influenced attitudes to traditional trade unionism. The traditional utilities which unions deliver to their members no longer mean so much, making people less inclined to join unions and pay dues.

During the boom times of the earlier phase of the growth of industrial society, union leaders fell into a monopolistic behaviour pattern of a technocratic nature. (A technocrat is defined as a person who takes a rational technical or economic attitude without regard to human, cultural or environmental values.) Monopolistic self-sufficiency and failure to appreciate other values make technocrats incapable of setting up the signalling systems and learning the lessons that a new situation requires. This is highly important from the standpoint of self-diagnosis and for the good of the enterprise. People who grasp these issues can easily fill the gaps in their knowledge and exercise excellent leadership through business cycles and structural changes.

People who are heroes in good times often lose the capacity for self-criticism. Conversely, the heroes of hard times persist in the same kind of behaviour that won them success and thereby create problems for themselves and the enterprises they lead. It should be the duty of boards of directors to consider the executive management of companies and organizations in the light of business cycle fluctuations and structural changes.

GOOD TIMES V. BAD TIMES IN RELATION TO THE COCE MODEL

In good times for companies, *customers* are almost always subjected to attempts by suppliers to expand their scope of delivery: new service contracts, new products and services. This also means greater freedom of choice as the customer becomes the focus of attention and is offered a host of new temptations. Suppliers tend to lose precision, making all kinds of offers that are not related to the customer's needs or decision-making patterns. In hard times, by contrast, customers are handled with greater precision. The cry of "Back to basics" is heard from suppliers, and price becomes more important as a means of competition.

Success, with rising profits or greater social recognition, often inspires euphoria among *owners*. They express 100% confidence in the executive management which in practice assumes a dominating influence over the running of the enterprise. Ownership becomes one long celebration. This applies to the principals of all types of organization, not just shareholding owners. In bad times, owners are faced with the need to analyse the causes in detail. Was the downturn the result of structural factors that the management could not have foreseen, of bad business judgement, or of a lack of ability to think in strategic terms?

Costs generally rise in good times under the influence of a number of factors. The two most important are the absence of pressure to be thrifty and investment in long-term aspects of the business which are not required to show a short-term profit. The enterprise feels that it can afford to spend money, including on ventures of a more long-term nature. In bad times personnel cease to be the most important resource and become, instead, the most important potential area of rationalization. Though the customer is still the prime consideration, he or she has to share primacy with costs and capital. Precision in selling and marketing reduces the sales cost per pound, dollar or mark of revenue. A clearer distinction emerges between "good" and "bad" costs, and companies begin to review their business processes and the value generated by units that make internal deliveries.

Good times give *employees* a fine feeling of success. Nothing motivates people better than feeling successful. The tangible proof of this often takes the form of higher pay and other perks like company cars, etc. All these evaporate in hard times. European industries have made cutbacks in manning, pay and entitlement to drive company cars, and non-commercial organizations are now doing the same thing, though the lead time there is often longer. The need for downward adjustment is one of the hardest things to accept. Memories are short too, so people always tend to extrapolate the current trend, whether it be upward or downward.

Try this exercise:

Is the trend of your business pointing upward or downward right now?

Go back ten years and analyse upswings and downswings. What did the management do right or wrong, too late or not at all?

In bad times, was the determination forthcoming to make tough decisions?

In good times, was there a central vision to guide strategy and operations?

Do the people in your organization have any idea of when the next upswing or downswing is likely to come, and, if so, are you prepared to meet it in terms of personnel, mind-set and organization?

12
Final Conflicts and Closing Reflections

In this final chapter I discuss four more important conflicts:

- Own money v. other people's money
- Business v. people
- Trade mark v. individual
- Structure v. process

OWN MONEY V. OTHER PEOPLE'S MONEY

This heading may seem superfluous. The subject has been discussed many times, especially by neo-liberal politicians in their criticism of the way the all-seeing, all-knowing State spends its citizens' money. However, this important theme, once the exclusive hobby-horse and virtually the private property of the conservative and neo-liberal right, has now also begun to be emphasized by political groups on the social democratic side. The performance gap between different countries in the way they manage their resources has become so blatant that it cannot be ignored by any intelligent observer. The economies of the European countries bear witness to this.

The conflict between managing one's own and other people's money can likewise be observed in the microcosm of businesses and organizations. The subject is closely associated with the matters reviewed in Chapter 8 under the heading of market economy v. planned economy. Large sections of the organized world exist in a planned-economy environment, which means that the value created is assessed by people who do not have a free choice between alternative suppliers and whose money comes, so to speak, from above. The money they spend cannot be related to utility or revenue – a situation which blunts a sense of economy in stewardship of resources.

Stewardship means planned and restrictive expenditure of resources that are required to suffice for a given purpose over a given period of time. Motivation for stewardship diminishes with the square of the distance from the source of the money. This applies to staffs in organizations as well as to functional links in a value-added chain.

The term stewardship, as used here, refers to the ability to achieve efficiency, i.e. the greatest possible value at the least possible cost. That ability varies enormously according to whether the costs are paid out of one's own or somebody else's pocket. This is the prime motivating force of businessmanship. All entrepreneurial business is run by people whose own money is at stake and who, therefore, have a strong incentive and well-developed ability to achieve efficiency and manage their resources economically.

It may seem obvious to point to the lack of such an incentive in people and organizations who manage other people's money. This, however, is the largest single factor behind the inefficiency, slackness and sloppiness so prevalent both in financial politics and in sheltered parts of companies and organizations. The following is an example from civil aviation, which admirably illustrates the inability of both nations and companies to manage resources rationally:

On 27 July 1994 the EU Commission gave the French Government the go-ahead to inject 20 billion francs of capital into its national airline Air France.

At the same time a 1.5 billion pound bail-out plan was approved for the state-owned Greek airline Olympic Airways, as well as a state subsidy of 750 million pounds to Enichen, Italy's largest chemical company.

The European Union (EU) disapproves of state subsidies in principle, but allows them in practice. Air France made a loss of 8.5 billion francs in 1993. The subsidy was made conditional on certain sacrifices on the part of the employees: a pay freeze until 1997 and the axing of 5,000 jobs. Air France was forbidden to use the money to subsidize other wholly or partly owned subsidiaries like the loss-making Air Inter, and was further forbidden to expand its fleet or its traffic by more than 2.7% per annum.

Once more Brussels repeats that this is the last bail-out it will agree to, though this is by no means the first time that the French Government has had to come to its flag carrier's rescue. Demands have also been made for privatization, though that is scarcely feasible at a time when the airline is running at a heavy loss.

Arguments can be advanced for giving a company one last chance to put its house in order. A company may have an importance in terms of employment and national prestige that far exceeds its commercial importance. The rationale of the French Government's actions must be sought on other grounds than those of economic efficiency. The prestige of political power is so important that it takes precedence over all demands for rational stewardship of taxpayers' money. What normal owner of a company would agree to an injection of capital on such terms?

The sad result of the intervention by the French Government and the EU Commission is that competition will be biased and that state subsidies to one company in one country will be allowed to erode the efficient operation of companies in other countries.

This decision goes against the whole spirit of the European Union (EU). It came, moreover, at a time when several countries were in the process of deciding whether to join the EU, which was particularly unfortunate. The EU's declared aim of rationalizing industrial structures has lost credibility.

It is all too easy for those in power to tax the people and use the proceeds – other people's money – for their own benefit. We have seen numerous examples of robber-baron states in recent decades. The rulers feather their nests while the robber-baron state sets up inefficient systems that increase transaction costs. Some examples are Mobuto in Zaire (who controlled a third of his country's GNP), Amin in Uganda, Somoza in Nicaragua and Marcos in the Philippines.

The same phenomenon can be seen in companies where departments that depend on centrally allocated funding are insufficiently motivated to manage the allocated resources efficiently; it is somebody else's money. This is why organizations are divided into profit centres where decisions on how to spend money and decisions on how to earn money are made in the same place.

People generally manage their own money better than other people's money. If it is our money we have an incentive to use it efficiently, to get value for it. Systems of rewards should therefore be linked as far as possible to ability to achieve efficiency and manage allocated resources optimally.

BUSINESS V. PEOPLE

Interest in people, and a passion for group dynamics and individual psychology, can be contrasted with interest in business, i.e. in setting and reaching goals and winning prizes in the form of profits, etc. The question of which comes first resembles the question about the chicken and the egg.

People in enterprises subject to criteria of efficiency are well aware that their only true security lies in running the operation efficiently, whether it be measured by profit or some other yardstick.

In enterprises without criteria of efficiency – and there are plenty – there is a tendency to regard the staff and its well-being as central and the actual business of the organization as a secondary matter. This is because the *raison d'être* of the organization is unclear; it is simply allowed to go on operating because it enjoys a monopoly or provides employment.

Aviation, telecommunications and steel production in Europe illustrate the problem. The people in these industries, their employment and their pay tend to be regarded as the primary issue and operational efficiency as a secondary issue. Events have proved time and again that this attitude is a many-headed hydra that is not easy to kill, even with the aid of new insights. The idea of efficiency is slowly gaining ground, even though progress is erratic – five steps forward and four steps back. It has, however, had a hard time finding a toe hold in the tax-financed public sector. Highly educated public servants fight a hard rearguard action against demands for resource accountability, reduction of deficits and priority ranking of operations.

The most truly humane personnel policy consists in running the operation efficiently and, most importantly, getting priorities right. Efficient management generates the necessary conditions for good personnel policies. The organization avoids the need for cutbacks, sackings, structural shake-outs and closures. The answer to the chicken-or-egg question is that the operative content of the enterprise comes first, with human resource management as an integral part of managing the enterprise. To this very day there are people in personnel departments who are frightened of the word efficiency. They put the "soft" parameters before the "hard" ones, reversing the polarity of the cause-and-effect arguments.

Some of the companies and organizations that enjoyed spectacular success in the booming 1980s illustrate this point. It is considered good form for leaders to be generous in giving employees and their efforts a share of the credit for success. Employees are then named the company's most important resource and everything in the running of the company can be attributed to human effort, be it choice of strategy, definition of corporate mission or generation of energy in the organization and motivation of all employees.

When things become more difficult, employees suddenly become the main area of potential rationalization. The efforts of groups and individuals have fallen short of what it takes to maintain efficiency, and employees are then regarded as part of the cost mass. This was demonstrated with exceptional clarity in formerly successful businesses that ran into difficulties in the 1990s. The songs sung in praise of personnel sounded hypocritical and false to many employees on the day when lack of efficiency led to personnel and pay cuts.

In European countries with strong trade union movements it is almost impossible to take corrective action in time. Bernard Attali, the head of Air France, was sacked by the French

Government when he wanted to make necessary cuts in personnel and pay. Scandinavian Airlines System has been trying in vain for years to push through improvements in productivity against the opposition of the pilots' unions; its cost per hour in the air is still extremely high compared with the world's more efficient airlines.

Leaders of enterprises sheltered from competition who proclaim the importance of personnel and who name promotion of women and union movement involvement as priority issues, have often proved to be out of touch with reality when the pressure of competition hardened, and, with it, the pressure for efficiency.

Operational efficiency is, thus, the real key to employee-friendly management in a world of increasing demand for efficiency. In the absence of open competition to act as a spur, one can resort to benchmarking to supply impulses for improvement and thus avoid painful correction of mistakes in which the employees are the principal sufferers.

TRADE MARK V. INDIVIDUAL

Executives tend to confuse their own personal success with the success of the trade marks under which they operate. People who work in successful organizations pre-empt part of the organization's success for themselves. There is naturally nothing wrong with being proud of one's company and one's own performance. The mistake lies in projecting the strength of the trade mark on to one's own self. It is easy to be deceived into thinking that success in a given position under a given trade mark will necessarily follow the same individual in another position under another trade mark.

In the great thinning of executive ranks that took place at the beginning of the 1990s there were many deposed managers who were chagrined to discover that assurances of undying friendship and praise for their personal qualities turned out to be hot air when they lost their positions and no longer had the trade mark to fall back on. Telephones stopped ringing, and people switched loyalties and broke earlier promises. Persons who had previously deferred to them now displayed a different attitude.

Regardless of what a particular individual may have meant to the success of an organization or the strength of its trade mark, the status of that individual instantly falls to a low level when his or her own name is the only trade mark left. This may seem self-evident in the harsh light of hindsight, but I have seen many examples of disappointment at the loss of presumed greatness and felt impelled to mention the matter in this book.

Success is difficult to explain. One of the reasons, of course, is that the demands on the time of successful people are so great that they must be restrictive in the number of issues with which they concern themselves. This tends to create an impression of arrogance and haughtiness. Another reason, however, is that success tends to seduce people into confusing the strength of their own trade mark with that of the organization they serve.

This is an unjust world, and leaders are not exempt from injustice. A run-down organization needs a Messiah figure to lead it out of the wilderness. After an intensive search, and perhaps a few false starts, the Board or other governing body finds a saviour who leads the organization to success, benefiting its customers, owners and employees. The leader succeeds in converting a tarnished trade mark into a shining one.

But the leader's fundamental error, which often leads to his or her downfall, is that of confusing his or her position with his or her own person. Personal success is seen in isolation from the situation out of which it grows. The leader tends to take an imperial view of him or herself which may lead to a dangerous and treacherous form of self-deception.

No one should deny a successful leader the success that he or she has achieved. At the same time, we must be aware of the risk of self-deception in confusing the success of the organization with that of the individual.

STRUCTURE V. PROCESS

A structure is the inward nature and makeup of something. In an organizational context the word stands for *what* is done. A process is a sequence of events as a result of which something is changed and developed. The term is used in an organizational context to describe the group dynamics and creation of insight needed to achieve the purpose of the structure, i.e. *how* it is done.

I could equally interchange the terms structure and process with organization. A strategy is a structure, a matter of doing the right things in the right order, while an organization in this context is a process involving the group-dynamic and individual psychological aspects required to bring about change.

Experience suggests that the leader of a process of change tends to favour either the structural aspects or the process aspects, even though the task generally requires both (see Figure 12.1). The choice is closely associated with the cultural pattern in which the leader operates.

The ordinate of Figure 12.1 represents varying degrees of focus on structural aspects – analysis, fact base and strategy. At the top the focus is 100% and all relevant analyses have been made, resulting in a ready-formulated strategy. Near the origin at the bottom, however, the fog is impenetrable. The quality of the analysis is assumed to increase as one moves up the ordinate, bringing greater clarity concerning the goals the organization wishes to reach and how to reach them.

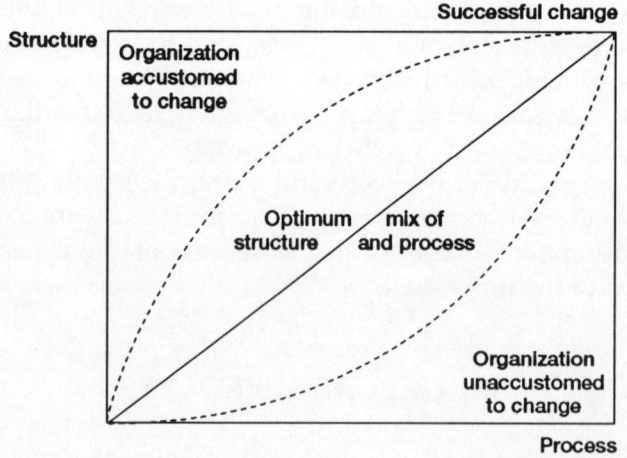

Figure 12.1 *Structural v. Process Aspects in Organizational Change. Source: Bengt Karlöf and Sven Söderberg,* Ledarutmaningen (The Challenge of Leadership), *Svenska Dagbladets Förlog, Stockholm 1989, p. 320.*

The abscissa similarly illustrates interest in and quality of work on the process aspects, i.e. the actual implementation. At the origin one has no idea of how to proceed, while to the right goals have been designed for every conceivable constellation of groups and plans of action for individuals. Everybody feels involved, and acceptance of the proposed change is 100%.

The actual goal, a well-thought-out strategy with a clearly defined course and deep commitment providing a platform for present and future success, however measured, is located at the top right-hand corner of Figure 12.1. The diagonal in the figure thus represents an optimum mix of structure and process, though this is seldom, if ever, achieved in practice.

If resources are devoted to resolving the structural issues and choosing the right strategy, this frequently happens at the expense of the process aspects. If engineers or economists are appointed to lead a process of change, they usually concentrate their efforts on the ordinate. Behavioural scientists, like organizational psychologists, tend to concentrate on the abscissa, devoting their energies to exercises in group dynamics without first plotting a defined course.

It is not unusual in organizations that are accustomed to change to find a curve like the one in Figure 12.1. The organization initially goes to work on structural aspects and considers process issues later. Such an organization accepts that the management has an analytical head start but is essentially concerned with the long-term good of the organization. Where change is an accepted part of the culture, management and consultants ought to be able to deal with process issues in a sequence differing from that used by organizations that are not accustomed to change.

An organization of the latter type has a tendency to overemphasize the process aspects. This is also true of systems where the pressure of competition is low, as in the tax-financed public sector. In such situations there is no acute demand for efficiency, and process issues can, therefore, take priority in a process of change. The result resembles a rain-dance more than a drive for greater efficiency, i.e. for more value in relation to productivity. The otherwise highly reputed consultant firm of McKinsey failed when it was called in to make changes at a large hospital in Sweden during the second half of the 1980s. The pressure for change in terms of efficiency was still not high enough there to let the McKinsey people move along the upper-left broken curve in Figure 12.1 which represents their standard operating procedure.

Thus, in environments where change is a foreign concept it may be advisable to spend a relatively large amount of time on the process aspects with a view to conditioning the organization to accept the idea of change. Bernard Attali probably made the same mistake when he attempted to reform Air France. Resistance to demands for efficiency, together with unfamiliarity with change, effectively blocked what were logical and necessary changes in the organization.

The conflict between structure and process, or strategy and organization, needs to be carefully considered in situations of change which are rapidly becoming the rule rather than the exception.

THE COCE MODEL AS A FRAME OF REFERENCE

A leader must relate everything to four important parameters:

- Customers
- Owners
- Costs
- Employees

The order in which they are listed here is not a question of priority; it has simply been chosen to make a pronounceable acronym. It is, however, obvious that all organized activity is based on satisfying customers' (or other users') needs, and that an enterprise is always started and operated by someone who owns it or holds a position of corresponding responsibility.

To reiterate, one of the central basic propositions is that "The purpose of all organized activity is to create a value which is greater than the cost of producing it." An enterprise is never created unless someone believes that this goal can be achieved within a reasonable period of time. One of the greatest problems is that the utility which an enterprise delivers is often judged by proxy and not directly by the users of its product or services. A

planned economy is based on the principle of proxy value judgements, as are all publicly financed services. If revolutionary theatre
groups are subsidized by the State over a long period of time, this
implies that somebody in a position of power is convinced that
their activities are of long-term benefit to society as a whole.

That is why the link to customers' needs via customers and
owners is so important. There must be people who are sufficiently
committed to an enterprise to work at it and accept the social and
economic risks involved. If this link is too weak, we will get false
demand which comes from irresponsible principals rather than
actual users. For these reasons it is natural that *customers* and
owners head the list of components of the COCE model.

The other two, *costs* and *employees*, are in many respects
simply means of accomplishing the satisfaction of needs and the
generation of a profit which are the aims of the enterprise.

Costs are a measure of productivity, i.e. input per unit of
output. Employees can be regarded as either a means or an end,
depending on one's point of view. In this book I have regarded
the enterprise as the prime consideration, with the employees as
a means of achieving the ends of the enterprise. It is, however,
quite possible to adopt a different and equally correct viewpoint
according to which the main object is to give people employment, in which case the enterprise in which they are employed
becomes a means to an end.

There are thus three important considerations to bear in mind
with regard to the COCE model:

1 We have left the handicraft stage behind; industrial and
   other enterprises are now organized with ownership sep-
   arated from management.
2 Such enterprises must always operate in competition with
   others and must therefore be efficient, i.e. they must be at
   least as good as similar enterprises elsewhere at creating
   value in relation to productivity.
3 Because of competition, employment of people must be sub-
   ordinated to the need for efficiency.

Humanity has tried for a long time to defend itself against the
need for efficiency by establishing islands of activity that are

isolated from outside-world competition, as exemplified by the communist states of the former Soviet empire.

In strictly material terms it is always possible to maintain a self-sufficient society shielded from the pressures of competition that prevail elsewhere. Psychologically, however, it has proved impossible, because people sooner or later start to envy the standard of living and the degree of freedom that they can see in the outside world. The standard countermeasure used by totalitarian states has been to try and conceal the fact that things are better on the outside, but they cannot keep their own people in ignorance of the achievements of others indefinitely. The closed system will eventually start to leak. Cuba is now a case in point.

In the COCE model the customer is regarded as an individual whose long-term needs must be satisfied. The owner must be able to live on the surplus generated in competition with other similar enterprises. Costs must be kept low to maintain a positive differential between the owner's desire for profit and the customer's desire for satisfaction, and employees must take pride in their work and be suitably rewarded so that they will continue to produce what is needed. Those are the fundamental parameters of the COCE model, the decisive criteria for the success of an enterprise.

Try this exercise:

Try to think of ways to ensure that units with little or no direct profit responsibility can be made to treat other people's money with greater respect. Is it, for example, possible to link payment to performance in terms of quality and profitability?

Do you or other units in your enterprise over-emphasize employee welfare at the expense of the enterprise itself? Are there clearly defined standards of performance against which people can measure the results of their work?

Does your organization have a tendency to over-emphasize structure in relation to processes between individuals and groups?

Do you, your boss or any of your close associates have a tendency to overrate personal achievement in a way that can ultimately be harmful to the individual concerned?

Index

Index compiled by Geoffrey Jones